FIRST
SH!T
VERSION

How purpose-driven entrepreneurs change the frickin' world

LISA BEAN

RΞTHINK PRESS

First published in Great Britain in 2020
by Rethink Press (www.rethinkpress.com)

© Copyright Lisa Bean

Contents

For my mum and dad, who made the incredibly tough decision to give me the best education they could.

Introduction

There must be more to life than this!

It took me ten years to write this book. Ten effin' years. Fair enough, I had some growing to do, but not that much. Bloody hell, not so much that I had to delay one of my major personal goals for a decade.

So why do we do that? Why do we delay our dreams and ignore the inspiration streaming through our consciousness? Why do we put off the abundance that is available to us right now in this moment? I mean it's like an extreme version of delayed gratification where we really *do* delay the gratification... forever! Maybe I'll call it *denied* gratification instead, ha.

Anyway, I'll tell you why we do it, seeing as you bought this book and it is kind of the point:

1. We don't really think it's going to work so we don't try – it's just too painful to fail. I mean what

will Roger from school think. (Roger who we haven't seen or heard from in twenty years.)

2. We really do believe we're not good enough – 'who am I to share what I know?', 'there are people out there who know so much more than me' – so we continue to consume other people's content instead of creating our own.

3. We think tomorrow really is going to come – 'Just one more day "catching up" on my emails then I'll begin'.

But what if it could work? What if it does work? What if we have everything within us that we need in order to grow into the person who can *make* it work.

What if we are enough? What if we're ready now? And what if there is a group of people out there right now waiting for exactly what we have to offer in this very moment? Because our story is unique and it resonates with them, now. Because our unique skill set matches their skills gap exactly and they're looking for us.

What if you took action today and put out your First Sh!t Version of the book, the online course, the event… **you**… in all your messy, authentic *this is me* glory? Because tomorrow is never guaranteed.

Just, what if?

* * *

I'm typing this introduction en route from the UK to LA. I'm off to spend a week with a business coach along with a dozen other badass women on a mission to change their lives and change the frickin' world.

The day before this flight, I was running around like a mad woman. I had a coaching call with a client, a discovery call with another client and a list of errands as long as an elephant's trunk, and I still hadn't packed. FFS (that means For Fuck's Sake if you're reading this, Mum).[1]

- Upload that vlog

- Reply to my graphic designer

- Paint my nails

- Walk the dog

- Book taxi to airport

- Call my video editor

- Eat*

- Change the frickin' world!

* Sometimes I have to put 'eat' on the list because, you know, life.

---

1   I swear in real life, so I'm swearing in this book. When I first sent the cover designs to my mum to see which one she liked best she replied, 'Ee, Lisa be careful. It looks like the book is called 'First Shit Version'. Is that a typo?' She laughed when I said, 'Nope. That's what it's called mum, ha ha!'

Alice, my beautiful girlfriend, had been asking me all day, 'Lisa, will you come in the jacuzzi with me tonight? I've turned it on ready.'

Now hang tight just a second. Yes, we have a jacuzzi... in an extension off our kitchen. At the time of writing, we live in a beautiful, magazine-worthy five-bedroom home in Tynemouth. There is a living room... a second living room (which we still need to buy furniture for), a guest room, we have an office each and Alice even has a yoga studio on the top floor.

Yup. We're living it up... As of three days ago, that is, ha ha. We literally moved two days before this flight. Because, you know... **life**!

So, I finished up my last call at 8pm, got into my bikini and slipped into the hot, bubbly jacuzzi for the first time. Ah. Bliss. In that moment, everything stopped. The jets blasted my back with a water massage. The lights changed colour from pinks to greens and danced in the steam. The voice in my head stopped.

Silence.

Presence.

Bliss.

Sometimes we forget how busy our minds get. How much that incessant white noise fills our head with worries and woes. And how much the world wants us to focus on lack and pain. No good ever came from that. Sometimes you need the contrast of presence just to notice how noisy you've let it become.

I sat back, looked out of the floor-to-ceiling patio windows onto the perfect square of grass in the garden and breathed. I wasn't thinking so much as feeling.

I felt abundant. I felt *expansive*.

I felt like anything and everything was possible right then in that very moment. Like this life I had been working towards had been waiting for me the whole time. Like there was so much more available. Like each of us really can have, be, do anything we want in our lives. Now.

It's the first time I really knew it in a physical, material sense – that anything is possible, and that you will always get what you ask for. Up until that point, I'd envisioned this life. I'd asked for it. I'd worked for it. And I'd told everyone it was possible because I knew in my heart it was possible. I was seeing the signs: growing businesses, more freedom, peace.

When word spreads

Four years earlier things were very different. I was in the midst of a six-year stint of depression. I was £100k in debt. And I was lost.

Crying to the sky one day, sat on the cold bathroom floor of my parents' house, I looked through the sky-light, beyond the clouds to the heavens and asked in desperation, 'There must be more to life than this?'

Aged twenty-eight, I was running two six-figure businesses: a graduate recruitment company and a digital marketing agency. I hadn't wanted either of those businesses. They'd happened, well, by accident. You see, I'd always wanted to be a coach. I wanted to help people change their lives. I wanted to help people get what *they* wanted in life. But I couldn't make it work for myself, so how could I help make it work for others?

Aged twenty-three, I had quit my job in London and moved home to build my first coaching business.

'Dad, I'm going to be a millionaire,' I proclaimed with confidence.

I failed. Miserably. And within three unceremonious months I was back in work, embarrassed, knocked, bruised. It turns out I had a thing or two to learn about business, money... and mindset!

Six months passed and then something crazy happened. I'd been telling a few people what I'd been up to. How I'd wanted to coach people. How I'd built my own website using a book I'd bought in Waterstones.[2] How I wanted to help people change their lives. Word spread and a woman I'd met approached me in my final few days in that job to ask if I'd build her a website for a business she was launching. It came at just the right time. I said yes! Oh, **hell yes**!

I worked for her for a month – building her website and helping her with her brand – and she paid me the equivalent of a month's wages. It felt amazing! I just got paid, working for myself! My new client recommended me and I picked up another website. And another. And another. Word spread quickly amongst business owners in the North East and before I knew it, I **had** to quit my new job in order to handle all the work in my business. Things escalated quickly and it wasn't long before I was hiring my first team member, and my third, and my eighth.

At the same time, I used what I'd learnt in marketing to relaunch my original coaching business… as a recruitment company. WTF was I thinking? But I followed the same approach I'd used to build the marketing

---

2   I reckon I could open up my own bookshop with the sheer range and volume of books I've bought over the years. Books on business. Books on art. Books on mindset. You name it – I've probably got it. I wonder, as you read this book, how many books you have too? Books are such a gift.

agency, an approach I now teach online, and things grew quickly again. We picked up FTSE 250 contracts, took on new offices, hired more people. And to sustain the growth, we borrowed money to pay wages, train up the team, buy new equipment.

To be honest, I got carried away by the buzz, the energy, the power of it all. It sucked me up like a hurricane and spat me out the other side. There's a name for this. My first ever mentor warned me about it when I was twenty-two. She said, 'Lisa, be careful of the offers that come your way. If you say yes to what people offer you, you will go off course. It's called "managed career drift". Instead – decide what you want and pursue that.'

Obviously, it's advice I never took... at first.

Wake the f up

And so, by the time I was twenty-eight I was depressed, £100k in debt and running two six-figure businesses I never wanted. I felt trapped. I felt like it was too late to change. I felt like my life was over and I'd **wasted it**!

I was twenty-eight, people, twenty-eight!

Sat on that cold floor of the bathroom in my parents' house, I couldn't seem to shake a thought that had been playing on my mind for weeks. I kept thinking to myself that *if* I died in that moment, no-one would have known who I was; they wouldn't have known the real me. I would have died alone with my dreams still inside me. A life unlived. A purpose unfulfilled. I imagined my funeral. People standing up to talk about how lovely I was, how talented I was, how much potential I had – the usual stuff. And I thought to myself that no-one would have had a truthful story to tell about me. Not the *real* me who had a vision, a purpose, a mission to change the frickin' world. Because I'd never told anyone about it. I'd never taken action on it. I'd never fully admitted it to myself.

Gabby Bernstein, an incredible spiritual teacher, often talks about her rock-bottom moment (in articles such as, 'How to Heal an Addiction', about getting sober from addiction at twenty-five years old) as being the moment when everything began to change for her. Our rock-bottom moments are important. They're the start of real transformation. And we should never deny someone their moment of transformation.

So that's when it happened – at my rock-bottom moment. The Universe cleared her throat and whispered, 'She's ready,' before smacking me in the face, punching me in the gut and shouting, '**Lisa – wake the f up.**'

And that's where this journey begins.

My promise to you

I have a feeling you can relate to this. Yes, your *details* will be different but broad strokes:

- You have a feeling you're meant for more but don't quite know what it is or, rather, you don't trust yourself fully to take the next steps.

- If you pass over,[3] people will stand up at your funeral and say lovely things, but you're not convinced they will truly know who you are because you haven't showed them yet, you might have even forgotten...just a little bit?

- There is something standing in your way – family, debt, fear, work, guilt, time – something that is keeping you locked in the current version of your life even though 'the calling' is getting louder and louder. You're finding it hard to rock the boat.

Am I close? Well, my friend, buckle in and prepare yourself. I'm about to take you on the ride of your life to truly uncover your purpose, find the courage to change your life and launch a business to make a living doing what you love.

Told through stories of my life and the people I've met on the journey, I'm going to show you that anyone, no

---

3   I wanted to write, *'If you die...'* but that felt a tad too direct. I mean, we're not even at Chapter One yet!

matter how difficult, dire or desperate their situation feels, can still rise up, take hold of their purpose and change the frickin' world.

The secret? Fuck perfection, let go of the bullshit beliefs you learnt from the people who live in lack, put out the First Sh!t Version of your *thing* and improve from there.[4]

You ready? Let's go!

---

4   Your 'thing' could be anything: a book, a talk, a vlog, a meet up, a recipe, a cartoon. Whatever you feel called to share, that is your *thing*.

PART ONE
WAKING UP

The Story Holding You Back

Yes, your childhood probably fucked you right up![1]

When I was eleven years old, I was sent to boarding school. Military boarding school. It had long been a dream of my parents to give me what they'd never had: a proper education. So, in September 1997, when the Spice Girls were on the rise and posters from Smash Hits magazines wallpapered most pre-teens' rooms, I packed my case according to the list supplied by the school and went on my way.

Five white shirts. Tick. Five pairs of forty denier navy blue tights. Tick. Two plaid kilts; one winter, one

---

1   Interestingly, this is the theme of a poem by Philip Larkin. I didn't know myself. My editor pointed it out and I searched out his name to read the poem. It's very apt. Search *This Be The Verse* if you're as curious as I was. I'll wait…

summer. Tick. Everything had my name sewn in. It was bizarre. My mum, who was a tailor in her early days, had sat down one evening and sewn in each label by hand. I know that every stitch hurt: she wasn't ready for this and neither was I.

I remember looking down that list of 'required items' and feeling deeply sad, unable to explain why. It was an adventure, to be sure, but I'd just returned from two years in a French-speaking school in Canada where hockey was played on ice and Céline Dion was the pop princess – everything seemed back-to-front to me. I mean, who the heck was Baby Spice?

What brought the first stream of tears was seeing my new hockey stick. Of all the things to be sad about, I was concerned about how I was going to hit the ball with this tiny, stumpy stick. My expectations of life were blown, and things were about to get worse.

My dad drove me to the school, took me to my bunk and made my bed. He introduced me to my roommate and before I knew it, he was gone. He thinks I don't know but I saw the tears burning in his eyes as he sped away. 'Be good,' he murmured in his broken voice. I ran back into the boarding house, straight into the toilets. I locked the door, sank to the floor and sobbed into my hands. Goodness knows how my dad felt, driving back six hours from Dover to Catterick that night.[2]

---

2   I don't think I've ever said this formally: Mum, Dad, thank you for my outstanding education, thank you for saving up for it before I

The first week was tough. I lay in bed at night and listened to the other girls crying into their pillows. Every so often, the 'matron' (the person who looked out for our wellbeing) would come round and whisper, 'Shh girls, get some sleep.' In some ways, I was lucky. Jason (my little brother) and I had moved every two years as kids and so we knew what it meant to pack a case and move on to a whole new world, make new friends and feel alone. But Jason wasn't here this time. I sobbed too, silently, until I fell asleep.

Bedtimes were scheduled each night and we were woken up every morning by a hand-rung bell. We showered, dressed and went to breakfast in a dining hall (think *Harry Potter*)[3] with the other 500 pupils. After breakfast, we did our weekly assigned chore – opening the curtains, vacuuming the day room, tidying the shoe room – and went to chapel where we sang hymns and listened to a sermon.

Lessons took place six days a week – Monday through to Saturday. Wednesdays, Fridays and Saturdays were half days and the 'free time' was mostly filled with sporting fixtures. I was on a couple of teams – hockey and tennis – and I joined a few clubs including horse

---

was even born, and thank you for the courage to put me in a school that made me who I am today.

3   The first book in the Harry Potter series actually came out when I was at boarding school. It was such a comfort to me to read about the students, away from home, lost in adventure. I devoured every book.

riding and pottery (as you do!) and so my time was always filled. It was better that way.

Homework was scheduled in, too – two hours every night after dinner. With life being so busy, we rarely had time to ourselves and, even when we did, there was nowhere to go to be alone.

On Sundays we did parade – full-on military parade with a marching band, a uniform and ranks. We paraded according to our house and the sixth formers were our NCOs (non-commissioned officers). There was even an RSM (regional sergeant major) on site, who taught rifle shooting (I joined that club, too) and continued the longstanding military traditions of the school. Each Tuesday and Thursday evening we did what was called 'drill practice'. Come rain or shine, we'd file out of our houses every single week to line up and practise moving in military parade formation.

'Left, right, left, right,' the NCOs would shout. 'Straighten your arms everyone, lock them out,' they'd bawl... 'Point your toes, come on, we're not going in until you get this right,' they'd yell, to smarten up our look. Things were competitive at school, and every NCO wanted the best house on parade.

I wouldn't have minded the whole parade thing so much, but I had a serious disadvantage. I couldn't straighten my right arm. When I was born, something went wrong. I was two weeks overdue and weighed in at 10lbs. My birth was very traumatic and both me and my mum came close to death. As the risk heightened, the doctors took emergency action.

It was too late for a C-section and my mum recalls looking over to my dad – who had pressed his body against the faded wall of the delivery room, white as a sheet and arms flat to the wall by his sides – as the doctor put his foot on the bottom of the bed, took hold of me by my arm and pulled with all his might. As he did, the tendons in my right arm stretched and tore. I was born paralysed down my right side and the doctors told my parents I might never recover. 'It's very likely she's brain-damaged, Mr and Mrs Bean.'[4]

For weeks after my birth, the specialist physiotherapist came to my nana's house where we were all staying and worked with my small, paralysed body. One day, after months of work, I moved my fingers and a miracle was declared. I think that's why I was always so close to my nana – we lived with her in those early weeks and she was there through it all.

As I grew up, I had operations to correct the position of my arm. They helped and I'm beyond grateful. My arm originally stuck out at ninety degrees from my body, as if I was constantly about to elbow someone taller than me in the face. The operations rotated my

---

4   Yes, my dad is Mr Bean. I think it's hilarious, too!

arm, so it sat closer to my side making it more discreet and much more functional. Fast forward to age eleven, though, and things weren't discreet enough.

The stories we form

I hated parade with a passion. It felt humiliating, pointless and painful. I dreaded drill practice every single day and it took place twice a week… but it wasn't nearly as painful as parade itself.

On Sundays we went *all out*. We donned 'military blues' – a smart dark uniform that was reserved especially for parades – with white shirts, white gloves and parade shoes we'd spend each week polishing. At 10am each Sunday, our NCOs would get us into formation, our hair bound tightly into buns under our berets, which boasted our family badge.

'AtteeeeeennnTION,' they'd shout, and our heads would jolt up from the 'resting position', our arms would snap to our sides from behind our backs and our right foot would lift and slam down next to our left foot. It was pretty impressive in truth. The noise of the polished parade shoes slamming to the floor in unison echoed across the school.

My problem was that my right arm wouldn't go behind my back and it wouldn't snap to my side either. It just sort of hung there, bent awkwardly and messily and it didn't go unnoticed, not by me and not by anyone else. How could it? We wore white gloves that seemed to shine out across the parade square, contrasting with the sharp dark colour of the uniform. It was like a beacon: look at her getting it wrong! Nightmare.

So, standing there one rainy day in November, I took my arm with my left hand and forced it behind my back. A sharp line of pain shot up my arm, traced along the scar from my operations and ran down my back. I stooped from the shock and a single tear rolled down my cheek as I affirmed to myself, 'Well done, Lisa. Now you blend in.'

And that's the very moment it happened: I formed a belief that was to hold me back for decades: 'Blend in, Lisa; standing out is bad, Lisa; people will stare, Lisa; you're different, Lisa; when you stand out, you let people down...' I actually thought this difference in me would stop me making friends, meeting someone, the works.

This was the first thing I learnt about change as I grew up: the stories we tell ourselves are just stories, but they are *powerful*, definitive even. These stories (or beliefs) are not the truth **but** we take them to be true.

Voicing your fears

In August 2015, I launched DARETOGROW in Manchester – the dream business I'd wanted all along. We had thirty business owners coming to our launch event and I was doing a talk – my first ever motivational talk with paid tickets. I was very anxious, not about speaking, but about being back on display, just like when I was at school. You see, the messages I'd drilled into my head on parade all those years ago were still playing in my mind like a ticker tape of doom, 'Blend in, Lisa. Don't put yourself on display, Lisa. Everyone will be looking, Lisa.' And, 'You'll let the team down, Lisa.'

And yet here I was, voluntarily putting myself out there. I just knew that, this time, I had to face it.

It was my first public motivational speech and I told the story in all its glory: the parades, the uniform, the white gloves. It was recorded and shared online and that evening I gave a huge sigh of relief. Voicing my fears like that, sharing my private story, was liberating, transformative even. That story had held me back for so long. I'd always felt a deep sense of shame around not being able to straighten my arm, like there was something wrong with me. Like I was 'less than'.

Recently, I was the keynote speaker at an event with over 350 female entrepreneurs in the audience. I stood up, moved about the stage and told story after story. After the event, I had a drink at the bar and met some people from the audience. One woman approached me and asked, 'So what's going on with your arm?' I explained the story. She looked fascinated and I could sense she wanted to reach out and move my arm to see what it could do. It turns out she was an energy worker and offered to work with me to help me get more movement. I laughed, 'Wait, no!' I said. 'This is part of my story now. It's my USP, ha ha!' She laughed, too.

What I've learnt, you see, is that we all have an imperfection like this; an idiosyncrasy we want to hide or disguise with an elaborate range of compensatory manoeuvres. Often, it's connected to a childhood or early memory: a moment when we felt deep shame, embarrassment, fear or abandonment.

Can you think of a similar situation in your own life? A moment where you felt shame or embarrassment or fear? A moment when someone shouted at you or told you how to behave or who you were? A moment when something happened that caused you never to repeat the behaviour that led to that moment ever again?

When we experience moments like this that lead to emotions of shame, guilt, fear or embarrassment, our fight or flight response makes a bold leap. It makes the situation feel life threatening. And when the experience is painful enough, it makes a 'command' in your subconscious mind: 'Don't do that again, it's not safe'. It forms a story that you believe will help to keep you safe from harm the next time… by playing small, by dimming your light, by shrinking into the shadows.

Maybe it's physical, like my arm. Maybe it's a feeling you have inside. Maybe it's something that happened to you or something you saw or heard. Maybe it's a secret someone told you that you're not allowed to share.

I've heard all kinds of stories from people over the years. It's a huge part of the online course I run; diving in to help people find the stories that are stopping them from expressing their authentic truth in the world. The problem is, we don't even know they're there. It's subconscious. It's a thought we literally hold to be true: it's a belief we think is fact.

As Jen Sincero says in her book *You Are a Badass*, 'The subconscious mind believes everything because it has no filter, it doesn't know the difference between what's true and what's not true.'

She says that if we believe our parents when they tell us a 'fat guy in a red suit' is going to bring us presents made by elves, then why wouldn't we believe them when they tell us money doesn't grow on trees, or we fight and shout in this family, or you're not smart enough, pretty enough, thin enough.

I remember telling Alice about the shame I'd felt over my arm one day. She laughed, looked at me with love and passion and said, 'Lisa, that's one of the sexiest things about you. Now pass me that book so I can see it again.'

In preparing to write this book, I surveyed over 100 people to find out why they hadn't already begun to build their dream life and pursue their dreams: 42% of people answered, 'Because I don't believe in myself.' Why not? At what point in your life did you make a decision about your potential? What is the story you've linked to your ambitions?

I'd love you to pause here, pull out a pen and journal and let your mind wander. What is the belief that's stopping you? What is the story that's holding you back? What do you think about yourself that won't let you take the next step?

And if you're struggling to find it, look for the problems in your life. For example, if you always find it challenging to stay in a long-term relationship – could there be a story there? If there is never enough money in your bank – is there a story there? If you have a vice you can't seem to quit – is there a story there?

As odd at this sounds, take a moment to look at the pain. Examine your secrets. Shine a light on the things hiding in the shadows.

Where you find resistance in your life, you will find a story. And stories have power. They will either push us forward or tie us down. We must therefore learn to craft the story we need to believe in order to move forward.

This is what this book is all about: how we shine a light on the stories we've held to be true for so long, how we recraft them in a way that lifts us up, and how we find the courage to build a life around the truth so we can help others do the same.

TWO

Giving Up Your Inheritance

One of the hardest parts of changing our lives is often the act of giving up our identities: giving up who we think we are, giving up the stories we've told for so many years. I mean we will literally start a fight to defend our impression of ourselves, even if that impression is self-limiting.

The spiritual lie

By the time I was twenty-eight, I'd built a pretty impressive reputation... on the outside! Two six-figure businesses. A growing brand. I seemed happy, optimistic, energised.

I was also quite quiet, introverted and easy going. I'd say, 'Yeah, sure,' and go along with other people's plans socially because I never really made plans of my own. I went to that event, saw that show, ate that food. Even if it wasn't my cup of tea, I didn't have the courage to speak up. I didn't want to rock the boat. I felt like I worked all the time and was lucky to have people around me who *let* me do that, so I should be fair and *let* them decide how the rest of my time was spent.

So that's how I lived my life: business, corporate, growing on the outside – trapped, stalling and frustrated on the inside. I mean, I even ate meat... and I was dying to go vegan, literally! I was living a lie. Not an outright lie, like my name is actually John and I'm Brazilian and I just told you it's Lisa and I'm British. No, it was more of a *spiritual lie*. Like, I wasn't *living my truth*. Like I knew I was made for something in this world but was completely ignoring that calling.

It's like I had a split personality: the side of me you saw (corporate, amenable, *gets in line*) and the side of me you didn't (purposeful, hungry, a raging dragon ready to burst free). But how can you ever be happy, flitting between these two personalities? How can you ever find peace when you're constantly playing a role in a game you don't even like?

The truth is, you can't. Happiness is uncovering who you are and finding the courage to build a life around it.

Years ago, when I was twenty-three and setting up that first (failed) business – the coaching company designed to help students land their dream job – I wrote a blog called 'The Sausage Factory of Life'. Somehow, I had realised very early on that we are all put through the same cookie-cutter mould of education. The teachers know best, your parents make the decisions and it's all about getting good grades to further your education and eventually land a high-paying job. It's the system.

For most of us this imprint burns *deeply* in our psychological make-up: it affects the way we think, the actions we take and even the very beliefs we hold. We need permission for everything. 'The system' is there for predictability and control.

The red pill

The system is not for everyone. Have you ever seen *The Matrix* from 1999? This cult classic Sci Fi film is based on the idea that humans are asleep, enslaved. The 'Matrix' in question is the world that has been created to keep the minds of humans docile while their bodies are cultivated for energy. Morpheus, a leader dedicated to the protection of Zion and the freeing of humans from the Matrix, gives Neo (the main character) a choice, 'You take the blue pill – the story ends, you wake up in your bed and believe whatever you want to believe. You take the red pill – you stay in Wonderland and I show you how deep the rabbit hole goes.'

In the film, the red pill would allow Neo to escape from the Matrix – to wake up and enter the real world. In contrast, the blue pill would lead to him staying in the Matrix living in a false reality.

I love that film. It is the perfect analogy for what is happening in life right now – the great awakening, the consciousness revolution. The beautiful thing about the analogy is Neo and the fact he even knows there is a choice – the fact he even knew to step back and ask himself, 'Is this it, does this feel right?' I love that moment when he finally unplugs from the Matrix, looks around and asks, 'Why do my eyes hurt?' Morpheus replies, 'You've never used them before.'

This is the power of perspective. One moment we believe everything we see, everything we're told, and then something happens. We learn something new. We read a new idea. We are challenged. And suddenly we see anew – our eyes squinting as we use them for the first time in the new, altered world.

The Matrix ends with Neo talking down the phone to an agent who is trying to prevent the change, with Neo telling him that he's going to show the protagonists, 'A world without rules or controls, borders or boundaries.'

I couldn't have put it better myself.

The system

Life has never felt right to me in the system. The system is built for mass production – mass schools, mass patient treatment, mass consumerism, you name it. And we've all been raised in it. To succeed in the system, you must play by the rules. You must conform.

No-one wants innovation in the system, not really. I spent five years outperforming every goal every company ever set for me and they loved it at first, but it was not long before I was told to 'slow down, Lisa' or 'watch your step, Lisa'. I even worked for a company that said, 'Only area managers can use black pens, everyone else must use blue pens.' I mean, WTF? God how I wanted to use a *red* pen!

There comes a time in your own personal story of development when your growth becomes too much for the system. Like a small potted plant, your roots begin pushing at the edges of the small brown pot they forged you in. They do not have a bigger pot for you and so you must slow down, stunt your growth in order to fit in. Use the blue pen like a good little worker bee! 'You can grow, sure – just make sure you grow in line with my expectations of you and in respect of my own comfort zone', so to speak.

For many of us, this is OK. This is the way of the world and we conform. We wait for permission. We seek approval. We ask before we try. As for the rest of us, we wake up, we take that red pill and we get the hell out of there.

Only, it is never really as sudden as that. For most of us, we battle with this internal conflict for many years, thinking, 'There must be more to life than this,' while we do the same commute, we stick out the relationship and we put our dreams on hold.

The truth is that there is a whole world of possibilities out there. But 'managers', 'parents', 'teachers' can't show you this bold new world. They like the old world too much and they don't even know an alternative exists. They haven't woken up to it yet. So to find it, you must go seeking it. You must find the courage to open your eyes and jump. Alone.

The pain-pleasure principle

You might have seen a blog that went viral years ago. It was titled *Regrets of the Dying* and was published in 2009 by a palliative care nurse named Bronnie Ware.[1]

She recorded that one of the biggest regrets of the dying is that they never had the courage or conviction to

---

1 Bronnie Ware later expanded her blog into a memoir, '*The Five Regrets of the Dying – A Life Transformed by the Dearly Departing*', which was translated into thirty-two languages.

break the mould and follow their own dreams: to forge their own life. Instead, they toed the line and ended up living someone else's life until it was too late. I don't blame them. Our values are engrained deep within us.

Science shows that we are driven, deep down, by one core principle: the pursuit of pleasure and the avoidance of pain. We will do anything to feel love, acceptance and security – the pat on the back from a boss, the approving look of a parent, the societal kudos of a pay rise. And we will do anything to avoid pain: a scolding from parents, judgements from colleagues, the embarrassment of a failed venture.

It is engrained deep within us. In fact, in most cases the only reason we are still alive is because of the love of parents and our community. When we are born, we are helpless. We rely on parents or our community or the system to feed us, clothe us. The more love we receive, the more care we receive. It is paramount to our survival.

Even in the most difficult of circumstances, we will adapt and mould our behaviour for a glimpse of love or attention, or for peace or security. This might mean learning how to play small, so we don't attract *unwanted* attention, learning how to put our own needs second so we don't cause a fuss, or learning how to sooth others (especially younger siblings) so they don't feel the pain we once experienced. We will find the smallest reason to stay rather than leave. Even though a situation hurts, *it's certain, it's known. And who knows what's out there?* This applies to relationships, friendships, jobs, where we live. Everything.

When I work with men and woman who have grown up in abusive homes or with alcoholic parents, I find the greatest breakthrough comes when they realise how skilled they have become at hiding in plain sight. They realise they have never asked for what they want because they've been taught they will *never* get it. They realise they take a lot of blame for problems in relationships because they've been taught it's easier than defending themselves. And they realise they have an incredible, almost superhuman power, to feel and dissolve tension in a room.

This is how we have been raised – to seek love and avoid pain – and so it's no wonder so many of us conform to the role we've been given. No wonder so many of us are trapped in mediocrity. Fit in. Do as we expect. Defy our rules and we'll cast you out...into the abyss!

But it does not stop the question from popping up does it?

Should I turn my back on what I know, on the security of my tribe, and go in pursuit of something more, something different?

This is perhaps one of the most painful and perplexing questions we ask ourselves as we grow. And it is our true human nature to grow: to expand, to explore, to break free of the limitations placed on us. Nature is growth.

Locked in mediocrity

For many people, this is perhaps the hardest decision they will ever face in life: do we stay put, grounded in what we know, safe in the life we've been given or do we break free, challenge what we know and risk it all to build the life we know we can live? Do we jump and build the parachute on the way down?

When these questions arise in us, they seem ugly, clumsy and terrifying. We feel odd, different. Often, the first place we turn to resolve this inner conflict is family and friends. 'I've got this idea,' we say. 'I want to make a change,' we venture. 'What do you think to this?' we ask.

Posing this question often represents the single biggest mistake we can all make. Unless your family and friends are great innovators, leaders, movers and shakers, then you are almost certainly asking the wrong people.

In fact, I am going to be so bold as to say that when the question first arises, you are almost certainly asking the wrong people. This is because we are an average of the people we hang out with most. If you have been toeing the line for life, so have they.[2] Don't ask them – you'll scare them, they will scare themselves and they will urge you to conform. The pain–pleasure principle will kick in and it will be game over for you. You will falter. This is one of the biggest lessons I want to teach people: your family, friends and colleagues' 'group think' will keep you locked in mediocrity. Nobody means to hold you back and it's not really their fault – they haven't woken up yet, they don't know you can choose the blue pill or the red pill. In fact, they do not even know the pills exist. They are in their plant pots, quite content to struggle away within the confines of the system and taking what they are given from the pre-set menu on offer. And your talk of busting out of here is making them feel very uncomfortable indeed.

No, the moment you realise there is a system and can check out of it to forge your own path in this beautiful world of possibilities, it is already too late to ask for their advice. To them you are destructive, challenging, weird... or worse: fanciful, silly. They like their world. It might not be the best, but they are safe, secure and happy in their own ignorance. To be frank, they like having 'someone else' to blame for their circumstances – the boss, their partner, the government – because then they don't really have to take responsibility and act. No,

---

2   Take a moment to consider your closest friends. Chances are, you are very similar. You wear similar clothes. You earn a similar amount. You have similar challenges. This is because we seek people like us to feel safe, to belong. One of the fastest ways to change your life is to hang around with people who have a result you want too.

no – it's far easier to complain and abide than to take accountability and act.

Success leaves clues

Don't get me wrong, sometimes I have longed to go back to that state of sleepy discomfort. Take a 'normal' job and blend in. But it's not possible. Once you are awake, you are awake – and you know it.

So, if asking your immediate network is the wrong choice, then where should you go for advice or guidance instead?

Tony Robbins, a great life and business strategist (perhaps my first ever and my biggest 'virtual mentor') says that, '... success leaves clues'. In video after video, he tells us that if we want to change our lives, then we must go and find someone who has already done it and model their behaviour.

This frustrated me no end when I first heard it. I thought I didn't have access to these people. I couldn't just call up Tony and say, 'Here Tony, can you teach me?' But I was wrong, I did have access to him. We all do. Successful people, the really cool people who love personal growth, want to bring you with them. They are awake and want nothing more than for us all to awaken to the joys life has to offer outside the system. They write books. They make videos. They create online courses.

Immerse yourself in their teaching. Read everything you can. Watch everything you can. Whenever you are driving, listen to an audio book. When you wake up in the morning, read ten pages of motivational, instructional content.

You are the creator

One of the most amazingly powerful principles I ever learnt is that I created my life. I am 100% responsible for everything I see in my life. I created it with what I know/don't know, with the mindset I'm currently operating/not operating, what I did/didn't do, who I know/don't know. Doesn't it make sense, then, that to get a new result I'm going to need new knowledge, a new mindset and new actions? And wouldn't it just be easier to ask someone who already has the result I want?

It's such a simple principle but it's hard to accept because it moves us from 'victim' to taking full responsibility for our lives. It's far easier to blame other people, then we don't need to change. But know this – you can change anything about your life *only* if you take full responsibility for the life you're creating now. If you don't, and you remain the victim, continuing to dwell on the past, then you leave yourself powerless to change.

I remember sitting in Alice's mum's house, reading *The Success Principles – How to Get from Where You Are to Where You Want to Be* by Jack Canfield (with Janet Switzer). And I was very upset. At twenty-eight, I was £100k in debt. I just didn't know about money. Well that's not strictly true. I *was* taught about money, but I was taught the poor person's version: money doesn't grow on trees, a good day's pay for a hard day's work, save, save, save and enjoy your money in retirement.

In the book, Jack Canfield says we must take full responsibility for our lives, 'most of us have been conditioned to blame something outside of ourselves for the parts of our life we don't like'. He goes on to explain that the only way to create the life of our dreams is to give up all of the stories that allow us to be the victim.

I got it immediately. Blaming my parents for not teaching me more about wealth allowed me to play the victim. It meant I didn't have to change. I couldn't. But the truth is, my parents couldn't teach me any more about wealth, they just didn't know any more. They hadn't been taught it either. They were taught that security meant getting a job, getting a mortgage and doing your time. So that's what they wanted for me too. But, if I wanted financial freedom, if I wanted true wealth and abundance, I'd have to learn for myself. And so I did.

The price of happiness

There is a price to this growth that isn't financial.

In 2015, I decided to dramatically downsize my marketing agency. It cost me around £100,000 to extract myself from the business I had built from the ground up. You see, I had borrowed heavily in order to grow. When I wanted to 'check out' and start again, the borrowing very quickly became debt I had to repay. To say I was broke would be an understatement. From that day forward, every penny I earned went on survival and debt repayments.

One day, my car (a beautiful blue Ford Focus my parents had bought me for my twenty-eighth birthday) broke down. This was the third time it had broken down in as many months and I just could not afford to repair it – not this time. The garage wanted £1000 to fix it. At the time, I was living with my parents (I was super broke, remember) and I was fed up. 'For fuck's sake,' I remember shouting. 'Fuck it!'

My parents were devastated for me. They were so confused as to what I was doing with my life, as was I, in all fairness. I had just taken the red pill and was making the clumsy, lonely transition from my old life to my new life. I didn't have a clue what I was doing or where I was going. I just knew I had outgrown my plant pot and, in fact, I didn't even want to be in a plant pot anymore! I wanted out and I was prepared to risk it all just for a taste of freedom.

'I'm going to buy you a new car,' my dad said to me.

'Dad, please don't,' I implored. 'I don't know how to handle money,' I said. 'If I can't afford a car on my own, I will have to get the bus. This is a lesson I need to learn. Please, don't buy me a new car.'

'Lisa,' he replied, 'I'm your dad and I'm going to help you. You need a car and I'm going to buy you one.'

I told him five times not to buy me that car. 'I won't drive it, Dad; you're wasting your time and your money. This is something I need to do.'

I wanted that car; I needed it! My clients were all over the North East and I had no idea how I was going to get to my meetings. I didn't want to alarm any clients, I had to be there. I needed the money! But what I needed more was to change my beliefs around money.

My dad bought me the car. A lovely little light blue Peugeot. He sent a text to tell me.

'Dad, I'm sorry but I won't be driving that car,' I texted him back.

He was gutted and he didn't understand. My mum was upset and confused. 'Lisa, we're your parents, we can help you and we want to – why suffer when you don't have to?'

What they did not understand and what I could not articulate at the time was that the car was just another plant pot. That car was saying, 'It's OK to spend more than you earn Lisa, your dad will bail you out.' I didn't want to be bailed out. I wanted to change.

My parents are lovely and so kind, but this is something they just couldn't help me with. I wanted to provide for myself, the Universe was serving up a hard lesson for me and I just knew that getting into that car would represent a step backwards. We fell out for a few weeks and I caught a train and two buses to my client meeting the next day. I have never been that broke since and I will never, ever be that broke again, but to learn that lesson I had to upset a few people, break a few moulds and make a few crazy-looking decisions.

When I first stepped out into this brave new world – 'a world without rules or controls, borders or boundaries. A world where anything is possible,' to quote Neo once again – I was terrified. I didn't really know what I was doing. I just knew I had to go. And I had to go alone.

Sometimes, you see, we 'stay put' because we feel guilty about leaving, about wanting more, about being different, but it is the people who stand up and step out into the unknown who create the future, who show others what's possible in their lives. We are innovators, creators and leaders and the world needs us in all our glory. Otherwise, we all just stand still.

The light in you

You have that light in you, don't you? That is why you're reading this book. For inspiration, for permission, for a way forward. And you feel stuck between the life you're living and the life you want. Between who you are and who you know you are destined to become. The truth is, you're on the path now. Your awakening is happening now. Your new life is available to you. And to claim it, you must find the courage to let go of who you think you are – who they told you, you are – and get ready to express the truth that is already within you.

As Dr Wayne Dyer told us, we are not human beings having a spiritual experience. We are spiritual beings having a human experience. And for that reason, we have chosen the *exact* circumstances we needed in order to grow.

You are being called, now, to shake off the labels, the expectations, the job title and rise up into the fullest expression of your truth. You're being called to build a life around the purpose within you. You're being called to lead. You're being called back home.

So, give up your inheritance – the values, the security blanket, the system, the very things that are holding you back – and go in pursuit of your own purpose in life. Look to your role models, read inspirational content, set goals. Look up and out, not down and back. Keep what lights you up and release what holds you back. This is your life and you are here to do something very special. But first you must shake off the expectations of others, let go of the excuses that have allowed you to play the victim, put your hand on your heart and ask, 'What am I here to do?' Then, find the courage needed to build a life around it.

THREE

Leading Flocks And Climbing Ladders

At the tender age of twenty-three, I left the world of work to set up my first ever business – a graduate coaching company.[1]

I had done really well on the graduate scheme I was part of; in fact, I distinctly remember feeling for the first time in my life like I fitted in on that scheme. 'This is something I can be good at,' I thought. And I was.

---

1   Well, that is if you don't count the very serious card making business I had when I was sixteen. I worked at a pet shop at the time and the owner very kindly let me sell my handmade cards by the till. Some days, I would make an extra £10 from selling my cards, which often equated to a 50% bump in my wages for the day! Not bad, not bad.

Whose ladder are you climbing?

I was the only graduate in the scheme's history to hit the top performance rating in all three placements. I was told it had never been done and it was impossible to do, not just by other graduates but by my managers on the scheme too. My response was to ask my managers exactly what they required of me in order to give me that top rating. I would type it up and go back to them, saying, 'So if I do this, this and this and demonstrate these behaviours... you'll give me a top rating?'

My managers would add in a few more things and I'd take it back and type up the extra notes. 'OK, so if I do this, will you give me the one rating?' I was obsessed – those ones would be my differentiator, my ticket up the ladder, my path to success.

As my third 'one' rating came in nearly two years later I was happy but, surprisingly, not elated. Tony Robbins says that, 'success without fulfilment is the ultimate failure' and I knew what he meant.[2] I was not truly happy because I was not fulfilled. I had climbed the ladder alright, but whose ladder was it and whose wall was it up against? I never even stopped to ask, I just put one foot on the first rung and began my rapid ascent.

---

2   Bill Carmody, 'Tony Robbins: I can tell you the secret to happiness in just one word', *Business Insider interview* (2017), www .businessinsider.com/why-tony-robbins-says-success-alone-wont -make-you-happy-2017-3?r=US&IR=T

I had learnt how to play the corporate game all too easily. I could see it for what it was. The path to success was simple – literally find out what your boss wants, do that with a smile on your face, whip up some support and credibility in your wider network (making it hard for your boss to hold you back!) and up the ladder you go. It's just another 'system' to figure out and play according to its rules. It's the great game of life.

By year three, I was in group head office, two levels and two salary brackets above most of my peers. It felt good, egotistically speaking, but I felt empty inside. I still had this feeling of wanting to help people, of wanting to teach people what I knew.

Then it hit me.

'I know,' I thought to myself, 'I could help other graduates to climb the ladder just like I have!' Almost immediately, I enrolled in a coaching training programme, got to work on the name of my new venture and began organising my launch event. My first company – a graduate coaching company – was born.

I became obsessed, finding more and more ways to complete my work quickly so I could continue working on my new business. I would wake up early, run in to work and be at my desk for 7am so I could get in a few hours of silent work in the morning, freeing up my afternoon to work on my business. One evening, I took myself to the Waterstones in Trafalgar Square and bought a book on how to build websites – Elizabeth Castro's *HTML 4 for the World Wide Web*. I was hooked. Within weeks, my first website was ready.[3]

Spurred on by my momentum, pumped full of confidence by my new website and pending coaching qualification, I quit my job. I had no money in the bank. No clients. And no idea! I felt compelled. And I followed that compulsion.

I remember calling my mum to tell her I'd quit my £50k job to follow my passions, 'You tell Dad, Mum, let me know what he says.' I was certain I would be a success, but I knew it would be hard to explain to my dad.

My parents were so proud of me. They'd scrimped and saved to give me the best education they could afford. And it had paid off! But I wasn't happy. I felt like a fraud: someone who had cheated their way onto the career rollercoaster with my corporate job, passing 'GO' each month and collecting the reward.

And so, within a matter of months, I had worked my notice and was hotfooting it up to the North East to move back in with my parents and pilot my first business idea properly.

---

3   I remember being terrified to put my new website live. I was worried I'd get so many enquiries and emails that I'd never be able to keep up with the demand! I needn't have worried. It was months before I won my first client through a friend-of-a-friend referral – nothing to do with my website. Isn't that how everyone wins their first piece of work?

Connecting the dots

They were such happy times. Naïve, first-time entre-preneurial bliss. I remember sitting at the dressing table in a spare room on the top floor of my parents' house (ahem, my new office), working on my website, developing my packages and listening to Choice FM on the radio.

I was writing blogs, building up my Facebook page and speaking to prospective clients about how I could help.

I loved it! But the bliss was short-lived.

Within two months it dawned on me that I had been a little overzealous. I'd won a few new clients (graduates who were paying me fifty pounds to rewrite their CVs) and I was spending a **lot** of money.

It wasn't long before my bank hit the big fat zero and I was back on the job-hunting websites. And within four months of leaving London I was back in paid employment – working for a small but growing con-sulting business in the region. I was so grateful for the job. But I was embarrassed, upset and confused. *Why hadn't it worked?*

On 12 June 2005, Steve Jobs, then CEO of Apple Com-puter and of Pixar Animation Studios, gave a com-mencement address to graduates of Stanford University. He told the new graduates how he'd dropped out of

Reed College but stuck around on campus for eighteen months, sleeping on floors in friends' dorm rooms.

As he walked around campus during that time, he noticed that all of the signs were beautifully written in calligraphy, a class available at Reed College. He decided to take the class and learnt all about typefaces, spacing and what makes typography great. He found it fascinating but it had no practical application at the time.

Some ten years later, when designing the first Macintosh computer, the beauty of the typography came back to him and he and his team designed it into the Mac.

He famously said during the address, ' ... you can't connect the dots looking forward; you can only connect them looking backwards.'

This is my dot-joining story and I bet you have one, too.

At this new job, I met a lot of interesting people. I got to talking about what had happened, talking humbly about my new website and how I wanted to be a coach. One woman I met seemed interested in what I was doing. She invited me for a coffee and asked me to quote her for building a new website.

I was flabbergasted. This amazing, corporate woman wanted me to build her a website?

I jumped at the chance and took the work.

By this time, six months had passed, and I was moving on from the consultancy. I built her the website and did some extra work on design and branding and got paid – nearly a full month's salary, a lot of money in my eyes. I was elated, especially when she recommended me and I ended up building another website, and another.

Each new client wanted something more: a logo, a corporate document, social media management, a full marketing strategy. Accidentally (and quite unintentionally) I had managed to create what was to become my first six-figure business: a digital marketing agency in the North East. The business grew quickly, and we tripled in size for three years running. It was insane, I was in business! The first dream I remember setting – to own my own business – had come true.

But… it was just another ladder.

As sales grew, so did our operations. I needed bigger offices, more laptops, better software… more team members.

During that fourth year, I fixed my eyes on the jackpot: a million pounds in sales. When I had left my corporate job in London, I had told everyone I was going to be a millionaire by the time I was thirty and hitting a million in revenue seemed an important step towards achieving this goal. I pushed and stretched both the business and the team. I took on bigger projects and hired more experienced team members. To finance the jump, I borrowed heavily – £30,000 from the Funding Circle and £20,000 from the bank for starters. On top of that, I had equipment on finance, and I'd fallen behind with HMRC payments.

Fuelled by my ambition to be a millionaire, I made the wrong decisions many times over and they drove the wrong behaviours in me. One night, going home from work, I suddenly thought, 'What am I doing and who am I doing it for?'

But it didn't stop there. I'd fallen into a trap: 'How can I make more money?' I'd always ask myself. And using the skills I'd learnt through the marketing agency, I relaunched my graduate coaching business as a graduate recruitment company. A mere three or four years after leaving behind my big London job to 'break the mould' and help graduates achieve success in their desired field, I had built a six-figure marketing agency and a six-figure recruitment company. I was going to work (my work, my business) but I was still in suits, I was still tied to a job. How was this any better?

My very first mentor had warned me about this very scenario when I was twenty-three; she called it 'managed career drift'. Without knowing who you are or what you want, you take what is on offer. You go for the promotion available. You start to climb the ladder and with each rung you climb, the salary, the kudos and the security become too overwhelming to leave, to let go. It becomes your path.

I can't afford my dream

This happens to so many people. They make promises to themselves: 'next year I'll leave to go travelling', 'when the kids leave, I'm going to set up my own business', 'once I've made my money in this business, I'm going to launch my dream business'. And they never do. It's too late – they've built a life that depends on that salary, they've become too attached to their reputation or they feel like it's just too late to pursue their passion, their purpose.

This does not surprise me. When we spend all our time and energy climbing someone else's ladder, we build the knowledge, skills and experience needed for *that* ladder; their ladder. That is why we do not have faith in our own ability to build our own ladders – we do not have the knowledge, the skills nor the experience. We have to build those attributes ourselves, over time, without being paid, without the promise of due rewards – and no-one wants to do this. Remember, we have been raised to value security, listen to the boss and fall in line.

Let me tell you something for free: *you'll never have the money you need to launch your dream business; you'll never quite have enough confidence in your ability to jump and you'll never have enough time.* And if you're waiting until 'you're ready', that is a false promise. You'll never truly feel ready to jump. You just have to trust... and jump anyway.

When destiny calls

Aged twenty-nine I was trapped. Gaining weight, broke and depressed – I was running from day-to-day madness like a headless chicken. I knew I was unhappy and wanted to change, but in my mind, it was **impossible**. I was far too high up that second (and third!) ladder with no safety net, no way off.

I remember being in the office one day and saying to Alice (then my operations manager and now life partner), 'I have to go home; I've just got to go,' and off I went in tears. The pressure had become too much for me. It was not the pressure of being in business: it was the pressure of living a life I no longer wanted. I was miserable. Waking up, going to work, coming home every day. I was in a rat race of my own making and I was trapped. My ladder was too high, and I was too scared to let go. I couldn't do it.

Alice was really concerned; she had never seen me like this. The next day she brought in a copy of a book she'd heard about on the Oprah Winfrey talk show, Paulo Coelho's book, *The Alchemist*.

I began reading the book and was instantly hooked.

It tells the story of a young shepherd who tends his flock. He takes care of the flock and the flock take care of him – they are dependent on each other. But he is not satisfied. Inside, he has a deep, burning feeling that he can be more, do more. He wants to go in pursuit of life's great treasure. But he feels torn between two options: *stay in the safety and comfort of what I know or take a risk and go in pursuit of my treasure.* Sound familiar?

It resonated with me deeply. *I* was the shepherd and my businesses were my flock! I loved my team and my clients; we had been through so much together and we had become reliant on each other. They needed me and I needed them. We were safe, we knew what we were doing, and things were moving along – I knew it would work out OK in the end. But I had that burning desire inside of me. I knew I was more than I was demonstrating to the world and now I had the language for it: I wanted to go in pursuit of my destiny.

Then a team member sent the full team a link to a talk by the late, great Steve Jobs – it was an extract from the talk I mentioned earlier, the 2005 Stanford Commencement. In this short extract, Jobs said he looked at himself in the mirror every day and asked if he would be excited for the day's activities if it were his last day on earth. If the answer was no for too many days in a row, it was time to make a change! He said: 'Remembering that I'll be dead soon is the most important tool I've ever encountered to help me make the big choices in life.'

This message had even more impact by the time I heard it because Steve Jobs had indeed passed away and it was in that moment that I realised how limited our time on this earth is. As the motivational speaker Les Brown says in 'Step Into Your Greatness Live', 'Don't allow fear of failure and the allure – the attractiveness – of playing it safe in life to draw you in. You can't get out of life alive you've got to die to leave here.' When you think about the fact we'll all be dead one day, doesn't that help you to reprioritise what you worry about?

Then, as if pushed by fate, the third happening in a trio of unusual events: I found myself slumped at the kitchen table one morning before my mum left for work.

'Lisa, this isn't right,' she said through her tears. 'You need help. I'm sending you to the doctor, no discussion.'

She called the doctors' surgery and instructed me to get dressed. I felt an ounce of relief as I pulled myself up the stairs to my room on the top floor.

I showered, got dressed and went back downstairs to the kitchen, heavy-hearted and desperate. My eyes were grey. The sparkle I once had, had left no trace.

As I walked the few hundred metres to the doctors' surgery, I struggled to quieten my mind. 'You're a loser Lisa, you're fat, why do you even bother?' It was a relentless broken record of abuse that one decent human could never say to another. But I ate it for breakfast, lunch and dinner. I was addicted to it.

Inside the doctor's office, everything was as expected. The old chairs, the corduroy, the stethoscope. How had I ended up here?

'How can I help you today?' he asked – a string of words he'd uttered hundreds of times.

I looked down to my feet. I was wearing HappySocks® – brightly coloured socks my mum had bought me. She said that if I wore them, I'd look too silly not to smile. The edge of my mouth cracked into a micro-smile.

'I have depression,' I murmured. My throat burned. My eyes filled up. And I lifted my head.

'I think I need help.'

The doctor was a nice man. He listened to my story for a few minutes, taking notes on his pad, 'Can't sleep? Can't get out of bed? Afraid?'

I looked to him, eyes wide and burning, waiting for the fix.

And that's when it happened.

As he muttered the words thousands of us have heard before in those anonymous doctors' surgeries, 'I'm going to prescribe you anti-depressants …' – I left my body.

I floated up to the ceiling like a helium balloon and looked down on the scene. There was a broken young woman desperate for help and there was a desperate older man unable to help at all. We came from different worlds. We had different challenges. And we couldn't find a bridge between us.

I watched the scene unfold and an anger filled the room.

'I don't want medication. It won't help. **I hate my life!'** My words bounced off the walls and I crashed back into my body.

Surprised and caught off guard, the doctor raised his eyebrows and widened his eyes.

'Oh!' he muttered, clearly shocked by the outburst that had come from this seemingly amenable young woman.

He sat back in his chair, rubbed his chin for a moment and then leaned back in to share his idea, 'OK. Go running. Go running every day for the next two weeks. The running will have the same effect on your body as the medication. Can you do that?'

I looked down again, embarrassed by my outburst.

'Yes,' I replied as I stood to leave, neither of us knowing the impact those two little words 'go running', uttered on a rainy Tuesday morning in a doctor's surgery in North Yorkshire, were about to have on the world.

The run

The next day, as the alarm sounded, I remembered my promise to the doctor. After an hour of tossing and turning, willing myself to get up, I managed to roll myself to the side of the bed and stand up.

I leant down and reached under the bed for my old trainers. I pulled on a running top, a jumper and some old leggings,[4] before digging around a few drawers to find some headphones – there was no way I could run while listening to myself desperately pant for air!

I'd dabbled in self-help books at this point and was starting to search out motivational speakers on YouTube to help lift my mood. On this particular day,

---

4   The leggings, incidentally, were in need of a very unfortunate repair. Having pulled on the Lycra and examined my appearance in a full-length mirror, I twisted around to see how my bum looked in them. We all do it! That's when I saw a big hole right down the seam. You could see my pants! Dear God, help, I thought, before I laughed at how ridiculous my life had become and proceeded on my run, with a now oversized T-shirt on to maintain my dignity.

I turned to a new speaker, Les Brown – a motivational speaker from America with a hearty laugh. Les Brown is an amazing storyteller. He was telling a story about a friend of his who'd asked him a question:

'What would you do if you found out you only had six months left to live?' he asked.

In that moment, I got an instant mental download. It wasn't a list of things so much as a feeling, an intention... a vision. I would give up my companies, move to Manchester (somewhere I'd always wanted to live), tell my now partner I was in love with her (that's another story), write *this* book and finally launch my dream business as a transformational coach and speaker and step out on stage to help people change their lives! Boom!

'Ha!' I laughed to myself, 'As if... '

Almost as quickly as I'd received the download, I'd dismissed it. Obviously, I was never actually going to sit my team down and make them redundant. I was never going to give up everything I'd built over the last few years. I was never really going to tell Alice I was in love with her! But destiny was calling.

The next question that came to me caused me to stop in my tracks, 'How do you know you haven't got six months left to live?'

That question felt like a near death experience to me. In that second, I experienced my own mortality. I realised that I might die with all of this still inside me. I'd leave this earth with my dreams, my destiny, unfulfilled.

'Knowing I'll be dead one day...' I heard Steve Jobs' words ringing in my ear. 'Fuck it!' I shouted. I turned on my heels, ran home and wrote down the list. The next day I walked determinedly into the office and told Alice what I wanted to do.

I had taken one step down the ladder. And in that moment, I changed my life forever. Could I afford to? No. Did I know how? No. Was I sure things would work out? No. On the other hand, could I continue doing what I was doing? Not for one second longer. It was time. The balance had shifted. Now the only thing more painful than the shift was the thought of staying where I was.

I rang my parents, 'Mum, Dad, are you sitting down...?' And I took another step down the ladder.

PART TWO
LIVING ON PURPOSE

FOUR

Ego And Other Addictions

Have you ever had a secret you were terrified people would uncover? I have. I've had a few.

The secrets we keep

One of my most shameful secrets emerged shortly after that run and the decision to downsize my marketing agency, start again and build a completely new and totally unrelated business. And life, for that matter!

You see, we had grown quickly as a company and, as you do when you're young, lost in your own hype and foolhardy with money, I borrowed more than I should have to grow more quickly than was wise. I wanted it all and was far too impatient to work for it! So, I borrowed it *all*.

The marketing agency had grown rapidly and, while this excited me, it also fooled me. If I had made it to six figures in just over three years, from nothing (and twice – I had two companies) then maybe I could make it to seven figures in another two years, even sooner perhaps? I could not wait to post that news story on LinkedIn. *Millionaire, aged thirty.* That was literally one of my biggest goals – and consequently my biggest trap.

Still high on the idea, I called the bank and arranged an overdraft of £20,000. Then I called the Funding Circle and negotiated a £30,000 loan with them.[1] These loans combined with finance options on the new Macs, a couple of personal credit card debts and previous director's loans (money I had put in to grow the company initially), brought my borrowing to well over £70,000. It was fine though; we were making well over £20–30,000 and sometimes £40,000 per month and I was comfortably paying the loans in line with the loan conditions.

The growth continued. But, as with all good stories, things didn't quite work out as planned. Pay rises. New offices in Manchester. Bigger offices in Durham. New

---

1   Of course, it's never as quick as that. You have to fill in the forms, get your end of year account statements from the last three years and do the dance of back and forth. All the while behaving as if you've got the money!

recruits. Consultancy fees to find the new recruits. I have to say; £50,000 is not nearly as much as you think it is when you spend it like I did.

Before long, the money was gone but the growth plan was in motion. As I said to my team, 'We've jumped off the edge of the cliff now and we've got to work hard to make it to the other side.' 'We'll make it, there is no alternative,' I added, channelling the stories of the commanders who 'burned the boats' (or burned the bridges) in hostile territory, thereby giving their armies no choice of retreat and every impetus to fight like their lives depended on it. I thought I was being inspirational, bold even. I wasn't, as I would find out very soon.

Start with 'Why'

But let us rewind a second. It's February 2015, six months before I was to make the momentous decision to give it all up, submit to a higher calling and start again. Alice (my operations manager at the time) and I were on a recce to Manchester, sussing out the city as a potential location for expanding the business. Manchester was always on the news as being the digital hub of the North, the best place to live in England. I felt a strange draw to the city and wanted to check it out.

Midway through the trip, we were walking through the financial district when a young man caught my eye. He was standing, shivering, in a suit holding a sign with his degree on it and urging people who walked past him to take his CV. I loved the boldness of it all. I loved the lengths he was willing to go to in order to secure work. I approached this young man and offered to buy him a coffee in a local restaurant to find out more about him. It ended up being a mini interview. I asked him to meet me at a coffee shop the next day. He was very impressive: confident, informed and driven but not in an obnoxious way. He was driven by a core purpose, a calling. I'd never come across it before.

I offered him a job and he started a few weeks later, working from home some days and travelling to our office in Durham once a week. While discussing business strategy during a team meeting, he showed me a video that was to change my life in ways I couldn't imagine. It was a video clip of Simon Sinek talking at a TED Conference. The theme – 'Start with *why*'.

In the clip, Sinek draws three circles – with each circle sitting inside the previous one. He explains that most companies, when trying to market their business, start with the outer circle first: what they do. They then move to the next circle in: how they do it. He explains that companies who we really connect with – those big brands we obsess over – do things differently. They start from the inside out: they start with *why* they do what they do.

I grasped the concept immediately. 'I must start with *why*,' I thought to myself. It was to be months before

I realised that we all have a purpose, a calling. Simon Sinek was just the beginning and thank goodness for him. He introduced me to the idea within a framework I could understand and relate to – business. I am not sure I would have grasped the idea had I heard about it in the context of spirituality first.[2]

Back to the moment of decision, then. I had jumped off the cliff bringing my team with me, I had clocked up £70,000 of loans and I was wondering what my 'why' could be. In fact, I was wondering a lot more than that...

Standing in your own way

What the hell is it all for? Why am I here? What is the point? You know that an awakening is just around the corner when these questions start filling your head as you eat your morning cereal.

So, there I was, aged twenty-nine: the founder of not one but two six-figure businesses, responsible for eight people, servicing multi-million-pound clients with the world at my feet. Why was I still so deeply unhappy? It felt like I was on the verge of everything and yet absolute oblivion in equal measure. It felt at that moment

---

2   To this day, I am very grateful to the young man I took for coffee for introducing that video to me, and I know he'll go on to do amazing things. Thank you if you're reading this book.

as though my life could turn on just a single roll of the dice.

By July 2015, things had come to a head and I felt like I was going crazy. It was like I was trying to take a French lesson in German – I did not have the right language to describe how I felt. Not long after this crescendo of uncertainty, I was taken to the doctors for my depression and was prescribed running. That's when I had reached for my audio of Les Brown and gone on that run; the one where that question, 'How do you know you haven't got six months left to live?' stopped me in my tracks.

Suddenly, as if by magic, I received the clarity I had been searching for. I knew what I had to do: get out of the businesses, pay off the debt and launch DARETOGROW. I had to follow my passion. But... there was a problem. Someone was standing in my way. Me.

I would not let myself do it. I was addicted. To my money. To my Managing Director status. To my businesses (and yes, I loved that, that was plural). To my reputation. To my own self-importance. To the whole fucking drama of it. I was totally and utterly addicted. I lived, slept and breathed for business, for success, for money. The dopamine, adrenaline and cortisol pumping into my system were fabulous stimulants. I wanted more. I needed a bigger hit. Hence the loans. Hence the leap. Hence the new, separate office I got all to myself. I mean, come on!

I needed to get out of my own head. I needed to stop and as they say, when the student is ready, the teacher will appear.

Waking up

Enter Eckhart Tolle.

Aged twenty-nine, Eckhart Tolle (who was to become an international bestselling author with his book *The Power of Now*) recognised he had lived in a continuous state of anxiety with extended periods of suicidal depression. Then one day, he woke up early in the morning with the most profound feeling of dread. Everything felt alien to him, hostile and utterly meaningless. In the depths of that despair he asked himself why he should bother carrying on with such a continuous struggle. He could feel a deep longing for annihilation, for non-existence.

'I cannot live with myself any longer,' he thought, over and over again. And then it happened. The breakthrough.

On that lonely morning as he lay awake and fearful in the dark while the trains passed quietly in the distance, he woke up. He became aware of his own awareness over the voice. 'Am I one or two?' he asked. 'If I cannot live with myself, there must be two of me: the 'I' and the 'self' that 'I' cannot live with.' 'Maybe,' he thought, 'only one of them is real' (p1).

And so began his journey, from the frantic and persistent ramblings of the ego to the higher power of *source energy*. He described this as the process of *waking up*: of breaking free from 'inherited collected mind-patterns that have kept humans in bondage to suffering for eons' (p4).

Yikes, what does that mean? Simply this: you are not who you think you are. You have been raised to believe you are your achievements and shortcomings, your past experiences and future expectations, your thoughts and your beliefs. You believe you *are* the voice that chats away incessantly in your mind.

But none of this is true. You are consciousness. You are *the witness* to those thoughts and not the thoughts themselves.

Michael A Singer gives a wonderful explanation of this in his book *The Untethered Soul*.

He explains how it feels to be lost in a movie: 'You forget your personal thoughts and emotions, and your consciousness gets pulled into the film.' You become totally absorbed in the drama. A sad scene comes on and you feel a stir of emotion. There is a tense chase and you feel the anxiety in your body. There is a love scene and your heart bursts open. Because you are focusing on these events, you react to these events. For a moment, you are experiencing the feelings as if you were right there in the movie.

But then you remember where you are. You're sat in a cinema, in between strangers. You can consciously observe, 'Oh, I'm in the cinema, watching a movie. These feelings are a result of what I was focusing on.'

And even though the movie continues, you can change the focus of your consciousness entirely to a book you read or an event you attended or a time when you achieved something wonderful. You have the power to shift your focus. And by commanding what you focus on, you can command how you feel and, as you will learn later – you can command what you attract into your life.

So, to bring this back to that incessant chatter in your mind. It's going on and on and on, on repeat. That's like being engrossed in the movie, only this time, you're focused on the *show* in your mind and you're *experiencing* the emotions of that *story*. If you keep focusing on the debt, you're going to experience feelings of lack, worry and fear and likely attract more debt into your life.

You don't want to do that. So pull it back. Become the *observer* of your thoughts. Witness that you are thinking about debt. And change the focus to something positive instead.

You might instead say on repeat, 'I can't wait to have more money in my life,' or 'I am very excited to learn

more about money and how it can flow into my life.'
It's a more positive thought and it will literally shift
your whole focus.

It's like learning you can switch the TV channel from a
horror to a comedy.

And yet so many of us continue to tune into the horror
because it's what we know, it feels permanent and a
lot of what we see around us encourages us to stay in
this state of lack.

As Russell Brand rightly says in his book *Revolution*, 'It
is extremely difficult to put aside a lifetime of conditioning. The rewards of thinking positively take time.'
And, it's very hard to give up your self-constructed
sense of self (your ego). You feel wedded to it. You say,
'it's too late' and 'a leopard can't change his spots'.

But it's not too late. And you can change your life. I'm
going to show you how.

Meanwhile, be mindful that most of what you experience in the world wants to keep you locked in a state
of lack. It's how people sell to us!

As Brand jibes in his book: 'Escape your life into this
PlayStation, mask the stench of your failure with this
fragrance.... Don't be you.'

Brand tells us that we've been sold the idea that freedom is being able to buy things to satisfy our desires

when in fact, freedom is the ability to *not* buy those things – because we are complete without them.

This is a profound thought. He's saying that we've been sold a dream; that success is being able to buy a car to say, 'Look how rich and successful I am.' In truth, success is feeling so confident in your true self that you don't need to buy a car to show anything. You are free from the demands of the ego and its need to 'show your place' in the world.

A journey to consciousness

Revolution is a wonderful and eloquent account of our conditioning to the system. We all adhere so beautifully to the rules of this made-up construct – the Matrix – despite the fact it is causing us all so much pain. I mean, how can it be that so many people are trapped in poverty and yet we cosy up in bed each night without giving their plight a second's thought? How can our conscious minds allow us to be so wasteful as if the world can sustain our need for more, more, more?

That's just the point… we're not conscious. Our subconscious is driving the show. Our need for love, gratification and reassurance makes us do things that literally go against the needs of ourselves, our species and the planet.

So where do you begin on your journey out of ego and into purpose, or out of a subconscious life to a conscious life? The truth is, you've already begun. It's because you're waking up that you picked up this book, that you've been following that new blog or asking yourself, 'Is there more to life than this?'

Yes, there is! But I'll be honest... the book will not give you the answer. The book is your guide, a process. You are the way and you already have the answers you need; you've known it for years: I'm just going to show you how to turn up the voice inside and turn down the outside influence so you can reconnect with those truths and find the courage to build a life around them.

You see, what I have learnt on this journey is that your purpose *is the way*, it's the enabler. It's your 'Ithaca', that destination that gives you a reason for your journey. Your ego is the trap, the barrier. As Ryan Holiday termed it in the title of his book *Ego Is The Enemy*. In fact, he's so afraid of succumbing to the temptations of the ego he had that very phrase tattooed on his arm. On his other forearm he had 'The Obstacle Is The Way' tattooed – incidentally the title of another (fabulous) book he wrote.

I was so very trapped in my ego, mostly because I did not even know it existed. I was tuning into the destructive voice in my head which said things like, 'Lisa – you're such a loser', 'Lisa – you're fat', 'Lisa – you've failed'. I said things like this to myself on repeat and I thought it was true. When I realised I could (1) Observe these thoughts and (2) Drown them out with positive affirmations, my whole life changed. And yours can, too.

Up until then, I was doing what that voice in my head told me to do. I had no sense of higher calling or purpose. I was caught up in the current of life, ashamed of my failings and promised salvation 'tomorrow'. As Russell Brand says, there always seems to be a condition to our happiness.

New conditions

In my marketing agency I used to talk a lot about anchors and sails. It doesn't matter how much wind you put in your sails, if you don't cut the anchors tying you down, you'll never get anywhere. The problem is, we're not always aware of the anchors holding us back: they're invisible; subconscious.

The condition to living your dream life and making a living from your passions, then, is two-fold: give up the old (cut the anchors) and take on the new (add more wind). Let go of who you think you are in your ego mind and get ready to embrace who you know you are deep inside – your higher self. Let me give you an example.

One evening in early 2016, my partner, Alice, took me to a Gabby Bernstein talk in London. I was in a major depressive slump and couldn't get through a day without crying. At the event, Gabby asked if anyone had any questions. Too embarrassed to ask, I sat quietly sobbing and I somehow felt Gabby notice. Right at the end Gabby said, 'One more, we have time for one more question,' and she looked at me. I put up my hand and asked her, 'Is depression real?'

Tears were streaming down my cheeks and I could barely form my words, but I didn't care. In that moment, I wasn't an MD, I wasn't a leader, I wasn't a transformational speaker, I wasn't a coach, I wasn't accountable to the world. I was Lisa and I needed help.

'Thank you,' Gabby replied. 'I'm really glad you've asked that question because so many people suffer with it.' She said it with such sincerity.

More tears, more eagerness to know ... 'What can I do about it?' I sobbed in response.

She gave me a very precious piece of advice that I have lived by ever since, 'Introduce new conditions – the only way to overcome an existing condition is to introduce a new condition.'

On the spot, Gabby gave me a free copy of her latest book and audio – *Miracles Now: 108 Life-Changing Tools for Less Stress, More Flow, and Finding Your True Purpose.* Alice and I started the CD the next night on the drive home from London and this new homework gave me strength like you wouldn't believe.

Gabby was right! You can't just 'give up' old beliefs; you have to train them out or drown them out. You have to replace the old with the new. I couldn't just stop being depressed, for example, but I could cut some of the anchors tying me down and add more wind in my sails to propel me forward. So, instead of drinking so much coffee, I drank more water. Instead of sleeping in, I forced myself on early morning runs. Instead of letting negative stories play on loop, I drowned them out with talks from motivational speakers.

One thing I started to do that has had a particularly powerful effect on my life was write a positive affirmation. It was like a story of all the things I needed to hear to feel good. Every time I became conscious of the negative thoughts in my mind, I pulled out the affirmation and recited it out loud until the negative thoughts dissipated. I still use it to this day.

This is the work. People ask me, 'Lisa, how do you change your life for real?' And I tell them:

- Give up the need to please others and tune back into your purpose, your truth, your dream.

- Find the courage to ask for what you really want in your life, set it as a vision and go after it at all costs.

- Get into vibrational alignment with your new life by focusing on gratitude, visualising it in your mind and believing deeply that it's coming. Because it is.

- Do the deep work needed to process the blocks and let them go, and act on the inspiration that comes to you to move forward. Cut the anchors and put wind in your sails.

Commit to this process and you can have, be, do anything you want.

Some people do the work and get incredible results. Others don't. None of us really want to face some of the things we have experienced that have caused us pain. That time we felt shame. That time we were abandoned. That time we were violated. We've buried the experiences. But what we don't realise is that before we buried them, our brains used them to make a judgement on life. You can call it a story, a command or a belief.

Don't rise up: when you stand out you feel shame. Blend in.

Don't take a risk: it's not safe for people to see you. Stay small.

Don't ask for what you want: your needs aren't important and he will leave you. Do as you are told, settle for what you have.

Often, we don't realise how much the stories we formed around these events are running the show. That's why we must do the work to move from ego to truth. We must ask why we're not stepping up. What's the story we're telling ourselves here? What are we afraid will happen? Nine times out of ten, there is one specific experience, often from childhood, linked *directly* to that story.

For example, the woman who was attacked doesn't want to write that blog or step on stage. She doesn't want to be seen. It's dangerous to be seen. 'Was it my fault?' she asks herself in pain. 'Will I be attacked again?'

The man who was told, 'Men are tough, pull yourself together and stop crying' doesn't know how to cry and process his emotions and so they leak out in other ways.

The woman who grew up in an abusive home doesn't want to ask for what she really wants. Her needs aren't important. 'I'm not lovable,' she tells herself, 'I need to stay out of people's way.'

We all have blocks. We all have stories. The work is in looking for those blocks, it's in processing them, it's in forming a new belief about what's possible.

That's what Ryan Holiday means when he says the 'obstacle is the way'. You can't just go around the trauma, you have to grow through it. And this is where counselling, therapy, coaches and circles come in. They're there to help you heal. If only you turn up.

Awareness is a gift

Growing up, I was often given shiny fifty pence pieces from my nana. She would tape them to a square of card, just bigger than the fifty pence piece itself and send them to me at boarding school. I'd spend hours trying to separate the money from that piece of card! Once, I had to hand one in at the tuck shop still wrapped in tape! She'd done a number on that one!

Whenever I told my mum she'd say, 'You're such a lucky girl, Lisa. She hasn't got much you know.' Or if I was at home and my nana gave me a five pound note she'd say, 'Aren't you lucky, Lisa. Share it with your brother.' Her intentions were pure and coming from a place of love. Love is all my mum knows. But, with that information from my mum I formed a belief very early on that 'I'm lucky to have money', 'I've taken it from someone who couldn't afford to share it', and 'I should share it'.

Fast forward twenty years and I massively under-charged for my services. I gave all my profit away in the form of new gear and pay rises for my team. I felt guilty when there was money in my bank so emptied it every chance I got. I wasn't doing this consciously. My subconscious money beliefs were running the show, and I was oblivious. It wasn't until reading *The Success Principles* by Jack Canfield that I realised I had some work to do around money.

EGO AND OTHER ADDICTIONS

It took me years to spot and remove those money blocks! You see, change takes time. And patience. And humility in buckets!

Be glad when the block appears and you become conscious over it. Then, and only then, do you have the chance to work through it.

The language of the Universe

This is the journey we must all go on – our awakening to the truth. We are abundant and abundance flows to us all the time. Our subconscious mind – our programming – is the block. But don't worry, you're not alone.

Everyone who has 'made it' in a way you respect (and I mean truly respect at your core) has embarked on this journey through ego and into consciousness: they have experienced the *'long dark night of the soul'*. Tune in and you will hear references to it everywhere. Have you seen the film *Avatar*? Do you know the story of Romeo and Juliet? Have you listened to Adele's lyrics? Take 'Rolling in the Deep', for example. I can't quote the song here but please, if you can, hit pause and go listen to it online. Listen to every word, especially the chorus. She knows, doesn't she?

I mean, do you ever have a moment when you're listening to the radio and a song connects with you on a deep level? That's because the writer *knows*. They have been on this journey and their words speak right to you, right to your soul. It's soul language. It's the language of the Universe. They faced their pain and turned it into magic. They got out of their story and 'stood *on* their story', as transformational speaker Lisa Nichols would say.

I didn't know this then. I wasn't able to read and hear the language of the Universe. I didn't know why I had to suffer so much. Despite this, I've always had this ability to 'step outside' myself and the situation at work and in business. To calmly watch a conversation play out. It's like I could remain objective in situations where other people would lose their mind, behaving in ways that seemed inexplicable. 'Can't they see how they're coming across right now?' I'd ask myself.

I could think one thing and do another. I called it 'playing the game' and the first company I launched was based on this game. As I've said, my intention aged twenty-three, was to quit my corporate job in London and show other graduates how to achieve success at an accelerated rate by playing the game. 'Success'. 'Accelerated rate'. 'The game'. 'Ego'. Ahem, I know.

What's funny is I thought I was unique. Like I was the only one who knew 'the game'. I wasn't.

The game

One day, before this all began, I'd stayed back in the office with Alice. We'd worked together for two or three years by this point and she had something about her I could never put my finger on. She was my right-hand woman. I'd do the sales, strategy and vision and Alice would do the operations, create the right atmosphere and coach a lot of the team (even though she never knew she was coaching back then). Essentially, I'd cause a ruckus and she'd calm it all down. I was sales and she was people. She's amazing with people – she gives them so much room to be themselves. Alice is the most non-judgemental person I've ever met.

So here we were, sat in the office at 10pm, and I had flip chart paper all over the walls. You know that magic whiteboard paper that sticks to the walls? I'd practically wallpapered the office in it, and I was drawing out structure after structure telling Alice all my plans and what I saw happening. (Yes, I know I was lost in ego, it's OK.)

Alice was always very gracious – she sat patiently listening to my ideas, my plans and my next moves. Funnily enough they almost always involved me stepping away from my businesses – selling them, hiring MDs, rolling one up into the other. What was odd, too, was that I always saw Alice in my plans. I just didn't know how or why. Just recently we were laughing about the fact I always tried to fit her into the structure charts, but she never did fit. We knew on a deeper level that we were supposed to work together but it didn't seem right putting her on a structure chart. We couldn't figure it out.

I loved working with Alice. She gave me so much space to think and ramble and explore, but sometimes I thought she could be too quiet, not voicing her opinions when I knew they'd add value. I felt particularly strongly about this when it came to team meetings.

That night, in the office, I was giving her some feedback. Casually, I was encouraging her to speak out, step up and lead. I wanted her to be more forthcoming, more outright; make more of an impression. I said it was important for her career and her progression. I knew she had something special, but it didn't always come out in front of groups.

I finished my rant and cool as a cucumber, she turned to me and said, 'Lisa, people have no idea who I am. My plan is so much bigger than one meeting or one conversation. People think I'm quiet and they think they can take advantage because they're bigger and louder and more corporate. But you can't take advantage of me. I know who I am and what I want and I'm working towards it every single day. Let people think what they want.'

BAM! It hit me like a ten-foot wave.

I frowned, questioningly, and looked at her in disbelief for what felt like an hour. All I could muster was, 'You know the game, don't you?'

She nodded.

My world spun and I knew right then I was in love with her. It happened that quickly.

Driving home that night I was in a frenzy. High as a kite, excited and eager – I couldn't wait to see her again the next day. But I was equally terrified and confused and annoyed with myself. I was Alice's boss and I was in love with her. Fuck.

For the next few days, I was very quiet and distant. I fell quickly into a depressive slump (my then go-to response for things I couldn't handle). It felt like this was another area of my life I'd now fucked up. I didn't have control of anything. It was like I was imploding and this last little piece of stability – my platonic, work-based relationship with Alice – had now collapsed too.

I had never felt so alone and, little did I know, I was about to hit rock bottom and start again. In every way. I was about to wake up.

Later that same week, I came into the office and told Alice I had a few things to take care of and wouldn't be in for a few days. My eyes burned with tears as I told her. I was pushing her away. We both knew it.

Another few days passed before Alice asked me to meet her for a coffee in Seaham Hall. I did. It was so good to see her. She has a warmth about her I can't explain. And that's when she gave me the book... *The Alchemist*.

Time for a change

Consuming everything I could from my new-found online mentors – Lisa Nichols, Gabby Bernstein, Tony Robbins and Les Brown – and reading every book I could find on purpose, the Universe, energy, and connection I knew it was time for change – my awakening. I turned to prayer.

It's funny because I recently rewatched the film of Elizabeth Gilbert's book *Eat Pray Love*. This quote sums up how I felt beautifully...

> One day, lying awake in her bed
> contemplating her life and her marriage, Liz
> had asked herself: 'Hadn't I wanted this? I'd
> actively participated in every moment of the
> creation of this life so why didn't I see myself
> in any of it?'
> – *Eat Pray Love*

She thought that the only thing harder than staying in that very situation was to leave. So she prayed to God, and her prayer went something like this, 'I'm in serious trouble. I don't know what to do. I need an answer. Please tell me what to do. Oh God help me please. Tell me what to do and I'll do it.'

The voice Liz heard told her to go back to bed.

The voice I heard that day, sat on the cold bathroom floor, told me to write a blog and tell my truth. To bare my soul and tell everyone the situation I was in and what I planned to do about it.

I was in debt. And I hated my life. I wanted to change it all.

I opened my laptop and the title spilled onto the page: 'Why happiness cost me £70,000'. I typed up the whole story and, with a deep breath, I posted it online and sent it to my clients.

I knew in my mind that the journey I was about to embark on would be impossibly difficult, yet I also knew that in my heart, it was the right thing to do. It seems so silly now, so small, but what I did that day was the bravest thing I'd done to date: I told the truth. I opened my laptop and typed up the secret I'd been hiding. I was in debt – a failure according to the system. I was absolutely up to my eyeballs and beyond.

Like Elizabeth Gilbert, I wanted to slip out the back door and start again, only I couldn't. I had to face my life. I had to make some new bold decisions. I had to take charge of my life and begin the transformation that comes from facing your truth.

As Elizabeth said in *Eat Pray Love*, 'Ruin is a gift. Ruin is the road to transformation.'

FIVE

The Purpose Of You

I know deep down in my core that we all have a unique and compelling purpose. A reason for being here. Something bigger than just 'get through the day', 'pay the rent' or 'put on a brave face'.

Broad strokes: we all share the same purpose. Our purpose is to become the fullest, highest expression of who we are, without the labels, without social conditioning and without the fear of failure and judgement. It's to awaken, it's to live consciously, it's to express our truth.

In more detail: your purpose is to be yourself; your true self. Literally, just be you and take bold action as instructed by your heart, not your head. Do what you know is right, even if it's hard or it puts you out of favour in your immediate circle. Speak your truth and use your voice even when you're scared, and people judge you. Share your knowledge generously and create a space where others feel safe to share theirs too. Create and inspire, don't compete and criticise. And do it with kind eyes and a warm heart, knowing all is good and all is right in the world because we are all on our journey back home to truth, back home to love.

That is your purpose. And it's my purpose too. Because we all share the same purpose.

What makes your purpose unique?

What makes your purpose unique isn't the nature of it (be your true self) – it's your story and how you communicate with the world. It's what you've learnt on your unique journey, it's how you connect with people and it's the way you show up in the world.

I was always very comforted by the words of Rebecca Campbell in her incredible book *Light is the New Black*. She wrote about being a spirit, remembering the day she chose her body, and how she was presented three choices for parents. As a spirit, she chose the best situation for her, based on the growth her spirit needed. I love that idea, that as spirits we're given a choice of families to join. Each family will create the environment we need to grow; the environment that will help shape us into *us*. Whether you believe it or not, I love the idea that *I* made *this* choice. I chose my life so I would have the perfect environment for my own growth. It takes me out of victim mode and into creator mode.

This is why your story, your struggle, your pain is such an important part of your journey. Everything you've been through has prepared you for this moment. What you have overcome so far has allowed you to develop wisdom, it's enabled you to build new skills, it has allowed you to grow into the person you are today. The friend. The student. The partner. The teacher.

Sometimes I hear people say they'd love to start their life over and go back to age twenty-one. That would be my worst nightmare. I'll keep the wrinkles forming around my eyes when I smile and I'll let my hair turn grey if I can keep my wisdom. Wisdom is a gift.

It's not too late

So even if you think it's too late or you're too old to live a life of purpose, it's not. And, my friend, this is what makes you perfect as a teacher. As you begin stepping into your truth and changing your life, you can connect with others who think it's too late and say, 'But look at me, I did it!'

When I stand on stage now in front of hundreds of people, when my videos are viewed online by thousands of people, when these words are read by you, it is my story that helps me connect with you. And that's why it was so important for me to write my book in this way; through the story of my life, not a list of 'to dos' and reams of advice you have to follow.

You won't remember the specific advice I give you. But you'll remember the stories I tell you, won't you? Remember my nana and the fifty pence pieces? Remember what happened on that parade square? Remember how I fell in love with Alice?

We are storytellers and we connect through shared emotions. We all know how it feels to hurt. We all know how it feels to be afraid. We all know what it's like to feel trapped. And when we see another person rise up against all the odds, start again and build a life beyond their wildest dreams, it gives us hope that change is possible. That growth is possible. That peace is possible. This is why I called my movement DARETOGROW. It's a challenge to rise up. It's a call to summon your courage. It's an invitation to grow into the next level. We have been called to rise up, reconnect with the truth and find the courage to build a life that enables us to continue this mission.

And just as my story may help you take the next step, your story will help someone else take their next step too.

I cannot stress this enough. What you've learnt on your journey is invaluable to someone else a little further behind you on the journey. You don't need all of the answers. You don't need to have it all figured out. You just need to be a few steps ahead. Then you can look back and share what you've learnt.

As I said right at the beginning of this book: there are people out there right now waiting for what you have to share in the world. And what's more is that there is a group of people *you* can reach that I can't reach. Just as there is a group of people I can reach that you can't. People connect with people based on shared experiences, shared circumstances, shared beliefs. Because my experiences, circumstances and beliefs are different from yours, we will help different people.

So, don't wait until you have it all figured out. You know enough to start sharing. And move deeper into purpose through action.

Your purpose is hiding behind the blocks

OK, so how do you do that? How do you connect deeper with your purpose?

Well, this is the first thing I want to tell you about the whole process and it's kind of annoying... you don't go searching for your purpose. It's already there – here. You were given it before you entered this world and it's there, inside you right now. In fact, by the time you've finished this chapter, you'll probably start to see evidence of it everywhere.

Your purpose is not a thing to be pursued, as Parker J Palmer says in his book *Let Your Life Speak*, but 'a gift to be received'. All you need to do to uncover your purpose is make room for it, create space, allow silence and listen. Well, OK, sometimes you need to probe a little and I'll give you some prompts for doing that at the end of this chapter.

You see, your purpose is talking to you all the time. It's that deeper voice in your heart that says, 'you can help that person', 'this isn't right', 'go on, do it', 'tell your story', 'just say it', 'there must be another way', 'wait, that's not fair'. The trouble is, we weren't raised to listen to our hearts or to trust our own gut. In the education system and in western cultures, we're raised to go in pursuit of the 'right' answer, to ask 'the manager'. We're told to study, to copy, to revise. It's all very *in our heads* and not in our hearts.

We are literally trained away from intuition, 'business isn't about emotion: take the emotion out of it', 'you can't make money from art, stick to maths', 'the board won't go for that: it's too wild'. We're meant to play it safe, right? Remember the plant pot from Chapter Two?

But how far has conforming gotten us? We might *listen* to people who have the 'right answers' but we are *inspired* by people who have followed their hearts.

I once found myself saying, 'we are all so ill-equipped for this journey', but that's not true and I corrected myself immediately. We are perfectly equipped for this journey. We've just been side-tracked by ego, by fear, by comparison. If we strip back the layers of limitation, conditioning and fear, we'll find our purpose, shining brightly in the dark. It is there now. And it always has been.

What this means is that we have work to do. We must start by offloading some of the baggage and many of the expectations and the 'lessons' bestowed on us by teachers, family, friends and managers. We must create room for our soul to speak to us and for our purpose to reveal itself. And to do this, we must become conscious of what is standing in our way.

We can start to do this by looking at our lives. Where do we experience conflict? Where are we unhappy? Where do we think, 'there must be more to life than this' or 'that's just not right'?

I often find the biggest clue comes in the form of injustice. When you see something happening that is perfectly legal but feels unjust to you, you are on the right path. If it's upsetting you, it's conflicting with your deepest sense of right and wrong.

Maybe you can't bear to see animals being treated in a certain way. Maybe you've seen something at work that just doesn't seem right. Maybe you find yourself coming to the aid of someone struggling in the same situation over and over.

Where you find that feeling of unrest, your purpose is talking to you. Where you feel called to act, your purpose is rising up in you. Where you feel overwhelmed with anger about an injustice in the world, your purpose is shouting 'act, it's time to act'.

Take a second to reflect on this. Where do you experience unrest in your heart? What do you think is unjust and should change? Where do you find yourself helping other people? There are clues in the answers.

Purpose vs why

People hear 'purpose' and think of their 'why'. Though the *why* of things is important, I think *purpose* and *why* are different. For me, your purpose is your truth. It's who you are. It's what you're here to do in the world. Your 'why' is your own brand of motivation: it's why you care enough to go on the *rather uncomfortable* journey of living by it.

For example, my purpose is to use my warmth, energy, and humour along with my experience in business to show people it is possible to make a living doing what they love. I do this in talks, through my writing and in videos.

That is my *purpose*. When I'm on stage sharing a story, I am expressing my true self.

My *why* is different. Whereas my purpose comes from a sense of power, my why comes from a sense of pain. I share stories to empower people because I ignored my calling and it led to six years of depression and many more years of unhappiness. Now, I can't bear to see people unhappy because they're living a lie just to fall in line. I want people to reconnect with their truth, use their voice to share their message and build a business to make a living doing what they love. It's possible. And people are doing it every day. So can you.

Now, I'm obsessed with giving people the tools they need to succeed as a purpose-driven entrepreneur in business. I'm obsessed with building supportive communities and empowering environments to help them do it. I'm building what I never had; what I wanted so desperately.

Living 'on purpose'

To live a life 'on purpose', you have to first accept that your purpose is already there. It is inside you. In fact, I actually believe it is you. *You'll never be happier than when living out your purpose because living out your purpose means being authentically you.* It might be hard, sure, and it will almost certainly involve a tremendous amount of growth, but it will feel fantastic. It will feel like home. Like truth. Like light.

When you live out your purpose, you stand on solid ground and it doesn't matter what other people expect of you or say to you. When you live out your purpose, their expectations fade away because you understand, finally, that expectations come from a fear mindset; from another person's need to control you and what you do.

When you uncover and live a life of purpose, you'll know what it means to live a life of higher conscious-ness. A life of light. A life of deep understanding. A life of love. Love and fear cannot co-exist, just as light and dark cannot co-exist. When you turn on the light, the darkness vanishes. *When you come from purpose, anything is possible.*

I really want to make this point because what I'm about to explain happens to all of us as we wake up. I hope that when it happens to you, you'll remember these words and continue with quiet conviction knowing that we all go through it. We must make it through because we have work to do in this world.

So, here it is. When you decide to change your life and build a life of passion, the people around you will not like it. Friends, family, and colleagues alike will find it deeply uncomfortable and they will try to stop you. Not all of them, no, but the majority of them will not get it and they'll try to convince you to stay as you are, for a whole host of reasons. Fear, mostly. Lack of understanding, probably. But also because they're not yet awake. When you wake up, it's like you can see the whole world so clearly: what makes people behave the way they do, why happy people are so happy and why people who cast the first stone are really just in deep pain themselves.

Their map of the world

When I was waking up, I had to deal with a lot of doubt and confusion from all angles. Some of it from the people closest to me. Like my dad, as I mentioned above. I love my dad to bits. I want to make that clear first of all. He and my mum have worked so hard their whole lives to give me and my brother the best education, working their hearts out to provide for us: to give us what they never had. As a result, we got to travel all over the world growing up, we both went to private schools and we've never been denied anything.

But... there is a downside. Or rather, a little resistance I had to overcome.

I come from a family of grafters. Get a job. Keep that job. Work damn hard. Don't get sick. We don't get sick. Work some more. Don't be late for work. Stay in that job for another year, it's a great salary. Work a little longer. Work hard. Did I say work hard? You get the point!

Because of this upbringing, I have an incredibly strong work ethic that I'm grateful for: a military work ethic. And, I'm very rarely sick. I love working hard, too... on things I love!

Imagine, then, when I called my parents to say I was quitting my job in London – my £50k job aged twenty-three. Or when I called to say my first business wasn't working and I was going back to work. Or when I called to say I was downsizing my marketing agency to uncover my purpose and follow my dreams and it would cost me £70k. The list goes on.

Fear. Confusion. Panic. Disruption. That's what they felt. In that order. Time and time again. They were programmed to feel that way. Their map of the world said get a job and stick at it until you retire – that's the key to 'getting through' in life. That's how you stay safe. I expect a lot of people work to that model but my model was different. I was in the pursuit of happiness.

When I told my dad my plans in 2015, he traced his eyes across the sky in a giant arc singing, 'Weeee'. I looked at him with a frown and said, 'Dad, what are you doing?' He did it again. He looked up and then traced his eyes across the sky in an arc from left to right as if following the line of a rainbow in the distance. 'Weeee,' he said again playfully.

'Dad? What are you doing?'

'Oh,' he replied, 'I'm watching pigs fly… '

Laughing at his own joke, he told me that I'd be successful with that strategy when pigs fly.

Remember – I love my dad, but I was angry. I took that to mean he didn't believe in me, but as time went on I realised that his model of the world was just different.[1]

---

1   I eventually let it go. But not before I bought him a pair of cufflinks: silver pigs with wings. The note said, 'They're flying now Dad.' We laughed and that was that. I hope he wears them to my book launch.

He had no context for 'making a living doing what you love', no role models in this space, no evidence it could work. He knew about grafting, falling into line, staying under the radar and sticking at it and he had thirty-five years of evidence to prove this model worked. And he had different drivers. He was a man in a nuclear family. His mission was to give us the security he never had growing up.

Uncovering your purpose is easy because it's right there waiting to be found, but it's hard because it inevitably leads to change. It rocks the boat in families, work and friendship groups. It's something new. It's something you can't quite explain. And that's why when you go on the journey (I expect you have already begun) you have to trust in yourself and not seek the approval of others. Not friends, not colleagues, not children nor parents.

Parker J Palmer, author of *Let Your Life Speak* captures this beautifully when he says, 'our deepest calling is to grow into our own authentic self, whether or not it conforms to some image of who we ought to be' (p12).

Spirits having human experiences

But even when you feel alone, know that you are being guided. As the late Dr Wayne Dyer said, we are all spiritual beings having human experiences.

I believe in God. I believe that God is another word for Source, Universe, Love, Light, Spirit. I believe that we come to earth to grow. When we die, we experience the full light of the Spirit which is love, lightness and knowing.

If you read any books about near death experiences, you'll read story after story of survivors feeling expansive and all-encompassing love along with a knowing that anything is possible.

I read a lot of books like this when I was waking up. I felt comforted knowing there was indeed more to life than this and that we were spirits having human experiences.

It helped me to believe that anything and everything is possible. It helped me to understand that we come to earth to experience hardship and challenges in order to grow.

Be open to guidance

When I first gave up my marketing agency and took on the debt, I was so afraid. I knew that what I was doing was *right*, but I was still afraid. In my darkest moments, I often prayed and always felt this incredible presence. I knew it was my nana.

My nana was an amazing person. I hardly knew anything about her, but I knew everything about her at the same time. She was from Liverpool and moved to Newcastle to marry my grandad.

When I was at Newcastle Uni, I'd go to her house in Howdon, Newcastle nearly every weekend and take her fresh scones and strawberry tarts from Fenwick's, the big department store in town. We'd put the kettle on, eat the freshly baked goodies and watch the Emmerdale omnibus. She'd ask me how I was, but she'd never pry. Mostly, we just sat in each other's company doing our thing. She'd be making little bets on the horses and I'd be writing or working on something. She'd always insist I had more tea. More biscuits. More everything and I loved it! I was so happy there in that little house, two up, two down. I could be 100% myself and my nana never said anything. She was always so proud.

My nana died when I was twenty-five and it still brings me to tears that I can't pop round for one more strawberry tart.

When I prayed for help in my darkest moments, it was my nana who came through, telling me it was OK and I was going to make it. I still pray to her now. Literally, before big talks, I sneak off into the toilets and pray, 'Please Nana help me remember my words tonight, help me be of service, help me turn up for the highest good.' I put all her energy into my charm bracelet and now when I look at it or hold it I know everything will be OK. It is OK.

I'm telling you: trust in your journey. You're being guided and the more you invite in guidance in the form of prayer and surrender,[2] the more you will receive.

So – when you feel like you're all alone, remember that the Universe wants the highest good for you. Direction is coming. Clarity is coming. More ease and peace is coming. But often we have to let go of what we have to make room for what we want.

As Andre Gidé wrote in his book *Les faux-monnayeurs* (*The Counterfeiters*) published in 1925, '*On ne découvre pas de terre nouvelle sans consentir à perdre de vue, d'abord et longtemps, tout rivage,*' translated as, 'One doesn't discover new lands without consenting to lose sight, for a very long time, of the shore.'[3]

It means you need to let go of who you are now to become who you know you are deep inside. You don't need the full picture before you make your next move, but you need to make a move to see what's next. And this requires trust, faith.

---

2   Gabby Bernstein's latest book *Super Attractor: Methods for Manifesting a Life Beyond Your Wildest Dreams* is a wonderful read on this topic – surrendering to spirit and asking for guidance.

3   This quote is often misquoted as, 'Man cannot discover new oceans unless he has the courage to lose sight of the shore' and is often attributed to Christopher Columbus.

Your purpose will unfold quite naturally and beautifully from within you. It's what your friends love about you. It's your favourite pastimes. It's how you make others feel. And often, sadly, it's the gifts and pleasure we deny or put last or bury or dismiss because they're unconventional or they won't make money, or someone doesn't approve. When we do this too much and too often, fear, anxiety and depression emerge because we've moved too far away from our purpose, our source, ourselves.

In the first half of our lives, then, we often spend a lot of time being someone we're not. In the second half of our lives, we begin the pilgrimage back to the source where our purpose is revealed, and we begin to live it out. Knowing this, I pray that I wake up much sooner in my next life!

Superhero powers

One of my favourite activities I like people to try in my online course is to email five people in their lives and ask this: what is my superhero power?[4] As in, what do you think I can do that is special and unique and amazing? That you count on me for?

---

4   If you're wondering why I haven't told you the name of it yet it's because it is literally called DARETOGROW/The Online Course. I am sure there is a better name out there for it. All suggestions welcome!

I got the idea from a wonderful (and magically short) book called *All My Friends Are Superheroes* by Andrew Kaufman. The author took everyone's strongest trait and turned it into a superhero power. For example, there is The Stress Bunny. If you arrive at a party and all of a sudden feel calm and relaxed, it's like The Stress Bunny is at the party, too. And there's The Seeker, who knows how to get to any place, even if they haven't been there before. And The Projectionist, who can make you believe anything they believe.

I just love that idea: that our greatest trait is our super-hero power.

You can literally do this exercise today. Email five people and ask them that exact question: the people around you can see what's special about you, even when you can't. Responses I've heard include:

- 'You make me feel safe' (told to a sexual trauma coach)

- 'You have a very calming presence and help me to relax when I feel frantic' (told to a meditation teacher)

- 'You're great at breaking the ice and making people feel comfortable' (told to an event organiser)

- 'I always feel it's possible when I speak to you – I just want get on with it' (told to yours truly, a transformational speaker)

As I've said, the truth is that you don't really *find* your purpose. It's there, right now. It's always been there. We were born with it, but as we grew up, we forgot it. Our connection to Source faded as we took on the values and habits and attitudes of our family, friends and idols. But it's right there! So, now is the time to stop clinging to your old life, your old belief systems. This isn't about perfection. It's a journey. Follow the trail like the shepherd in *The Alchemist*. Like I did.

How to uncover your purpose

To help you on this next step of your journey, I would like to share five simple exercises that helped me dig deep, tune in and uncover my purpose.

EXERCISE ONE – THE FREE WORLD QUESTION

Complete this sentence: 'In a wonderfully free world, everyone would feel empowered to...' You can replace 'feel empowered to' with 'feel confident to' or 'feel free to'.

For me everyone would feel empowered to make a living doing what they absolutely love and it's as simple as that.

Here are some examples to help:

1. In a wonderfully free world, people would feel free to love who they want

2. In a wonderfully free world, people would feel empowered to use their voice to tell their story

3. In a wonderfully free world, animals would be free from cruelty

4. In a wonderfully free world, people could live anywhere they wanted

Once you have your sentence, you can begin to ask: how might I have an impact on this?

EXERCISE TWO – ELEVEN POWER QUESTIONS

Here are some of the top questions I've used with coaching clients over the years to help them reconnect with their purpose. Take a moment to answer these eleven power questions. Get your favourite drink. Turn off your phone. Get out a clean sheet of paper or page in your journal and scribble away.

1. If I knew I couldn't fail I would…

2. If I wasn't afraid of what people would think I would…

3. If I was given a year off, fully paid, I would…

4. My secret fantasy is…

5. What topic can you never get enough information on?

6. What do you love doing so much you'd do it for free?

7. What do people thank you for most often?

8. What annoys you most in the world?

9. What would you get out of bed for at 6am on a Sunday?

10. If you could start all over again, what would you do this time?

11. What books and magazines are you drawn to over and over again?

EXERCISE THREE – YOUR SUBCONSCIOUS MIND

Before you go to sleep each night, really focus on this question and let your mind work on the answer while you sleep. You can adapt the question but be sure to phrase it in a positive way to get a positive outcome.

'What is my purpose?' or 'What am I here to do?'

EXERCISE FOUR – CHILD'S PLAY

What we did with our time as children can be a massive clue as to our purpose on earth as we did it for the love of it, before we worried what people thought of us.

1. What was your favourite game as a child?

2. How would you spend your time as a child?

3. What are your fondest childhood memories?

4. When you were a child, what did you want to be when you grew up?

5. What did you often find 'unfair' as a child?

EXERCISE FIVE – FOLLOW YOUR BLISS

This week, book in an old hobby or activity you love but haven't done in a while. If it's a big hobby and time is tight, find a creative way to do something similar or on a smaller scale. For example, maybe you used to love walking with friends, hosting movie nights or taking photos.

Remember, we all have a unique purpose. It talks to us all the time but as Parker J Palmer says in his book *Let Your Life Speak*, we must be patient, calm and still. He likened our souls to wild animals. You don't go charging into the woods shouting and expect to spot a tiger. Instead, you must sit quietly at the base of a tree and wait, '… the creature we are waiting for may well emerge, and out of the corner of an eye we will catch a glimpse of the precious wildness we see' (p7).

Your purpose isn't a goal to be achieved. It's a gift to be received. It's already in you. Call it what you like: integrity, light, purpose.

Just get quiet and let it unfold.

SIX

The Abundant Mind

On 17 February 1997, Jim Carrey, the actor and comedian, told Oprah on *The Oprah Winfrey Show* that he had once written himself a cheque for ten million dollars 'for acting services rendered'. He had written the cheque back in 1992 and had given himself three years to cash it in.

Thinking about what he wanted, he told Oprah, 'I would drive home and think, "Well, I do have these things and they're out there I just don't have a hold of them yet but they're out there."' He had done this – visualised what he wanted – since 1985 and things were about to change for him. His desire came not from his vision for a greater life alone but from an intention deep within; an intention to alleviate the pain his mum experienced from rheumatoid arthritis and depression.

He wanted to show her that her life mattered. Her life mattered because she had created him, and he mattered. He wanted her to be free from her pain and so, as a young kid, he would spend hours trying to make her laugh and then he'd go into his room with a pen and paper and try to figure out what life was all about.

One day he read a quote from Buddha, which said that all spirituality is there to alleviate suffering. He got it instantly – he knew that his purpose was to alleviate suffering with humour, and he remembered thinking to himself, 'I'm aligned. My purpose is aligned with this.'[5] It became the vision for his life: to make a living doing what he loved; doing what he had a natural affinity for – comedy.

With his purpose and his vision aligned – alleviate suffering by making people laugh – he carried that cheque for ten million dollars around in his wallet and just before Thanksgiving in 1995 he found out he was going to make ten million dollars shooting *Dumb and Dumber*. His vision for his life had come true and he'd achieved it by living his life's purpose.

Jim Carrey's actions show us the secret of the Universe in motion: set an intention, act as if it is coming and let go of your obsession with the *how*. Trust, and it will manifest.

---

5   Eckhart Tolle, 'Jim Carrey On The Power Of Intention', YouTube (2010), www.youtube.com/watch?v=8qSTHPABoHc

Believe it to see it

Try putting it this way, and as Dr Wayne Dyer says, to bring about what you want in life you must *believe* it to *see* it rather than see it to believe it.

Let's say you wanted to be a writer and publish a best-seller. If you believed it were possible, wouldn't you be writing today? The opportunity is coming so you'd want to be prepared.

If you wanted to be a coach and believed it were possible, wouldn't you be excitedly building your website and preparing your coaching packages ready for your first call with a prospective client? Because that opportunity is coming.

If you wanted better health and believed it was coming, wouldn't you be planning the things you can do with your improved health? Because that day is getting closer.

And the more you can do to get into vibrational alignment and build a container for the manifestation of that dream, the sooner it will appear in the physical plane.

Even if you don't feel inspired to write or can't see how a new client can find you at this early stage, doesn't it feel better to get excited about the *prospect* than to rule it out completely?

As Henry Ford said, 'Whether you believe you can do a thing or not, you are right.'

How you feel matters. What you focus on matters. So, if your dreams seem too far-fetched to be believable, reach for a more believable idea you can grasp today.

I can't wait to feel inspired to write.

I can't wait to decide what kind of coach I'm going to be.

I am so excited to focus on better health.

Think on what you want. Because, in the words of Rhonda Byrne, 'what you think about, you bring about'.

The power of thought

That is the secret of the Universe and understanding it is critical to building your dream life. It's known as the Law of Attraction – the idea that we can attract into our lives whatever we focus on through the power of thought.

It sounds simple. And it is. That's why I misunderstood it when I first came across this secret in 2011 in a book aptly named *The Secret* by Rhonda Byrne. I was twenty-two years old and was living in London at the time. It was about a year before I'd get the notion to quit my job and launch my own business. My best friend had recommended the book to me. Her mum, who was a nurse, had told her about it. 'Everyone is raving about it, Lisa,' she told me.

The idea was completely new to me: ask for what you want, 'release it to the Universe', act as if it is so, practise gratitude and, sure enough, it will be attracted to you as like attracts like. So, ask for money and cheques will appear through your letterbox... I asked for a lot of things back then but the main thing I remember asking for was... money, of course. And lots of it. I wanted to be a millionaire by the time I was thirty.

Having read *The Secret* I loved the idea of vision boards, where you cut out pictures from magazines that depict the things you'd want in your life: the car, the house, the partner. I didn't make one at the time, but I did do things like edit my bank statement in Photoshop. I changed it to show an amount of one million pounds in my current account which, when you think about it, is quite ridiculous because if I had a million pounds, I'm sure I'd be putting it to better use than that!

I asked for other things, too, and as year after year went by, I never really got what I wanted: wealth, financial freedom, the car, the house. But I wasn't one to sit around waiting. While I had a wish list of what I wanted, I began working away on my dreams.

My hard work paid off. As I've said, by the time I was twenty-seven, I had built two six-figure businesses and was working with multi-million-pound clients. I had forgotten all about *The Secret* and the Law of Attraction, and instead focused on the growth of my businesses.

Things were looking good, but something didn't feel right. I was depressed. Personally, I was broke even though my companies were bringing in a lot of money each month. And, I had this niggling feeling in my heart that I wasn't where I was supposed to be in life.

The courage to build a life around happiness

Have you ever had that feeling? On paper everything looks good and you know you should be grateful for what you have only, you're not. You can't be because, for some reason, you feel trapped by what you have and where you are in life. It's not what you wanted and now you're stuck. But you can't complain. It will upset people and you'll look ungrateful. That's how I felt. Stuck.

In my third business, my dream business, I had created this model to show my coaching clients. It was a picture of two overlapping circles, a sort of Venn diagram. Above the circle on the left it read, 'What you are, have and do'. Above the circle on the right it read, 'What you want to have, be and do'.

I'd get clients to fill it in. They'd write down what they already had on the left and what they wanted on the right. If what they had was in line with what they wanted, I would ask them to write it in the middle where the circles overlapped.

I'd say, 'When "what you have" and "what you want" overlap you're happy, content, aligned. When they don't, you're not and you experience longing, desire and sometimes even a sense of anger!'

This has evolved for me more recently. Now, I know happiness to be finding out what you were born to do and finding the courage to build a life around it. It's not even about acquiring it – often the pursuit of that desire is enough when you're working diligently and knowingly towards your goal. As human beings we're always on a quest for something. We're happiest when we have a goal and we're making steady progress towards it.

Seeking expression

Recently, Alice and I boarded a flight to Ibiza. Alice was hosting her first ever retreat abroad and I was going along to support her.

Owing to my blatant obsession with reading, I popped into the airport *WHSmith* before the flight and a particular book caught my eye.

It was completely black, with the title set into the cover in, what seemed like, an even deeper black. It was beautiful. Simple. Classy.

I bought it, along with some sweets and drinks for the flight.

By the time I'd landed in Ibiza, I'd read the book. I couldn't put it down. It felt familiar. It felt universal.

It was called *The Science of Getting Rich*, first written in 1910 by Wallace D Wattles.

The book is an instructional guide for the attainment of wealth using the Law of Attraction.

In the book, Wattles tells us that becoming rich is an essential part of living out our potential. We need money to eat, to learn, to travel, to experience life – 'to make the very most of yourself' (p68). Providing, as he insists, that our purpose harmonises with the purpose that is in all of us. As in – providing we intend to lift others up on the journey.

And he gives us 'the exact science' for making it happen.

As I flicked to the introduction of the book, I laughed when I read that this is the very book that Rhonda Byrne (author of *The Secret*) was gifted in 2004. Lit up by the wisdom Wattles imparted, Byrne dove into Wattles' research and studied his philosophy. Within a year of reading his book, she had produced the film *The Secret*. Her work brought Wattles back into the light.

Wattles wrote that 'we are subject to the urge of life, seeking expression, which ever drives us on to know more, to do more, and to be more' (p68).

And guess what he advised we need in order to 'know more, to do more, and to be more'? Money, wealth, riches.

We are seeking expression, just as the seed wants to burst into the flower, we want to be all that we can be. And it's hard to deny money is going to make that whole process a lot smoother!

It is funny because Alice and I often joke we were happiest when we were broke! There was something so magical about having a mission with all the odds against us. When I think back, it's not being broke that we loved. It was the new opportunity we had to blossom into all we were meant to be. It felt like we had the chance to start again. When you hit rock bottom, the only way up is *up*.

The trouble is that a lot of us never hit rock bottom. We idle somewhere just shy of the rocks. We stay in a job that is *just* bearable. We cling to a relationship that is *surely* better than being alone. It seems we'd rather endure the pain of what we're experiencing than risk the pain that comes with the *unknown*.

And this is why Paulo Coelho writes in the introduction to *The Alchemist* that when we go in pursuit of our dreams:

> '... intense, unexpected suffering passes more quickly than suffering that is apparently bearable; the latter goes on for years and, without our noticing, eats away at our soul.'

Coelho knows that the pain suffered in the pursuit of our dreams is acute but passes quickly. The pain we suffer when we resign ourselves to living an average life is more bearable, so we make no changes. But it eats away at us and makes us bitter.

I know that feeling. My life back in 2015 hurt but I guess it didn't hurt enough. But as Esther Hicks – an American speaker and author who channels words from a group of non-physical entities called Abraham – says that if you don't listen, the signs will get louder and louder. And if you ignore the signs, they'll get louder still.

You see, when you stray too far from your intended path (your destiny, if you will), your heart will tell you and the Universe will send you signs. They'll be small at first, but they'll get bigger and bigger until suddenly they're like a brick wall saying 'seriously – you're going to ignore this one?'

For me, my grave state of depression was my brick wall. There were small signs along the way. I knew I wasn't supposed to be running a recruitment company or a marketing agency, but I thought it was too late for me then. I'd made my bed and had to lie in it. Right?

Wrong.

That's when it happened – you know – the Les Brown run, the Steve Jobs video, *The Alchemist*. And so, I put down my books on strategy, operations and profit and picked up books on getting over depression, manifesting your dream life and change. I gave up business shows and networking and attended seminars with Gabby Bernstein and training events with Tony Robbins. I stopped writing about marketing and web design and started writing about purpose and how to build your dream life. I even started writing my book – the one you're reading right now.

The idea of dying with my story still inside me moved me in ways I'd never experienced before, and I started asking myself four very important questions – almost daily:

1. What do you want to be celebrating twelve months from today, Lisa?

2. How do you want to feel each day, Lisa?

3. What do you want to create in this world, Lisa?

4. Who are you here to become, Lisa?

Lately, I've been asking myself a more specific question. I like to imagine I'm in a boat, right now, out in the open sea. Every morning when I wake up, I ask myself: am I pointing in the direction of my chosen port or am I drifting? As Wattles directs: 'as the sailor has in mind the port toward which he is sailing the ship; you must keep your face toward it all the time' (p52). Once I correct my focus to get back on track, I ask: *and am I sailing with a smile on my face?* The second question is important because you can't get what you want with action alone. Imagine writing a chapter of your book in frustration, or replying to a client while feeling bitter? You have done the task, but was your intention right? Feelings travel in words. Intention travels in action.

You see, *what you intend for your life is what you get*. If your intention is to 'get by' or 'just pay the bills' then that's all you'll get. If your intention is to achieve great wealth or financial abundance, then that's what you'll get. Your vision for your life is your future. What you do today is creating your tomorrow. And the life you're living today is exactly what you expected for yourself not that long ago, good or bad. You will always get what you ask for and always get what you expect.

Let go of the *how*

And here's the crazy thing. You don't even need to know how you're going to make it happen. You just need to decide *what* you want to happen and believe it is a done deal. I'll give you an example.

I had given up on the idea of random cheques landing on my doormat, like it said in *The Secret*. I decided that you could set the intention, sure, but you still had to work hard to make it happen, *right*?

The Universe is always working to bring you what you want and if you can let go of the *how*, you will leave yourself open to more possibilities.

Not long before finishing this book, I started to reconnect more powerfully with the Law of Attraction. My business had grown significantly and in one year alone, we'd more than quadrupled the revenue from the previous year. I'd hired two people, taken on an office and launched a whole new programme.

For a moment, I felt out of my depth. The changes had happened so suddenly, and I felt a bit of imposter syndrome creeping in. Can I do this? Can I manage this? I messed it up the last time, what makes this any different?

I turned to prayer, I leant back into gratitude and I restarted my journal entries.

One day, I felt guided to go to the bookshelf and pick up a book – *Money and the Law of Attraction* by Esther and Jerry Hicks. I'd started it before but never finished it. I dug back in and within a few pages I felt immediately and powerfully reconnected to the Law of Attraction.

The book reminded me that nothing is more important than feeling good. And the best energy for manifesting our dream life is the energy of joy, of expansion, of gratitude.

As Hicks reminds us, 'When you remember that you get the essence of what you think about – and then you notice what you are getting – you have the keys for Deliberate Creation.'

Influenced by the teachings of Hicks, I introduced a new, deliberate practice. I bought an A5 notebook and started to record all of the abundance that was already flowing to me every day. I wrote down the day a friend paid for my coffee. I noted the payment I received on time from a client. I even took note of the wonderful comments and feedback I received online.

Then, quite out of the blue an old client reached out to me and said she'd like to send me a gift to say thank you for the work we'd done together months ago. I gave her my address and a few days later, a lovely package of vegan chocolate turned up in the post with a thank you card. I noted it in my new abundance diary.

No sooner had it arrived that I won a new client, again totally out of the blue. And then I picked up four new speaking opportunities, totally unexpectedly. I hadn't gone looking for them. I hadn't pitched. They just called me and asked me to speak on their stages.

And this is where things got trippy.

I recorded it all in my new abundance journal and continued to focus on the abundance that was flowing to me, using gratitude to drown out any fears or worries that crept up during the day. When I woke up each morning, I started my day with journaling, I read a chapter from *Money and the Law of Attraction*, I prayed for guidance and I said thank you for what I had in my life.

Then one day I woke up and, after my morning ritual and cup of tea in bed, I checked my email. Out of the blue, I'd made three sales of a course I'd added to an affiliate website two years ago!

'Alice, you're not going to believe this,' I said as I sat up in bed.

I explained what had happened and even wondered if it had been a mistake. Is this possible, I wondered? Can it really be so easy?

After my shower, I got dressed and logged into the account. I'd made $200 in my sleep! I spent an hour updating the text and links to make sure everything was working for my *new clients* and noted it in my abundance diary. That day I made two more sales. And another the next day. Within four days, I'd made $600 in sales from a course I'd forgotten was there!

And guess how the money is deposited? Via cheque! Yes, a cheque was about to land on my doormat in a completely unexpected way.

I was flabbergasted. And my belief in the Law of Attraction was strengthened again.

So, let me ask you: what do you want? What do you expect? Because the Law of Attraction is always working and *what you think about, you bring about.*

Dreams that gather dust

In December 2016, I submitted my book proposal to a publishing house in London. I was confident I'd hear back from them.

One month went by, and another. Then three then four. I submitted my manuscript to agents and thought about sending it to other publishing houses, but I'd lost a bit of steam. I was so close to being out of debt, I was happy for the first time in my life and I was living the vision I'd set for myself only eighteen months prior: I had money again, I had built a new business on my terms and I had time to read and write and bake! My circles had aligned for a moment.

I put the thought of my book to one side for a bit as it was driving me crazy. I closed my vision book, stopped practising gratitude formally and just went with the flow. As days turned into weeks and the weeks turned into months it was suddenly January 2018. I had taken my foot off the dream pedal and allowed myself to coast in comfort.

Lying awake one morning, I reminded myself that when you stop striving for what you want, what you don't want will grow automatically. It reminded me of something Tony Robbins had said on stage at the 'Unleash the Power Within (UPW)' event we'd attended in LA, 'If you don't stand guard in the garden of your mind, weeds will grow automatically.' It was something his mentor Jim Rohn had told him.

'Weeds have grown in my mind,' I thought to myself. 'I can never stop striving for the life I want.'

So, what would I be doing if I had secured a book deal, I asked myself? Well, I'd be finishing the book. Putting on talks. Building my connections with the people I can help. I'd be getting ready to go on tour, to promote it. But I wasn't doing any of that. I'd stopped writing for years! Not a new word written for my book, not a new event held. *Nada*. My dream was just sat there, gathering dust and all the while I was waiting for it to manifest.

Have you ever done this? Asked for something and maybe even done a bit of work towards it but then stopped for seemingly no reason? Sometimes we're scared it will never happen, sometimes we don't see results quickly enough and in some cases we're actually scared it will happen! So we stop working towards it and weeds grow in its place. We slip back to our old lives, old patterns, old habits. That's what I did. I changed my priorities. Instead of prioritising my new, dream life I began prioritising my current life: safety, security, cash-flow.

I kept saying to Alice, 'As soon as I get caught up with my work, I'll get back to writing,' but by the time I had caught up I was so tired and drained that I couldn't bear the thought of writing. The energy I was emitting was the *total opposite* to what I wanted to attract in my life.

'Something has to change,' I thought to myself. 'But what? Where do I begin?' I thought back to the major changes I'd made in my life a few years earlier. 'What had I been doing?' I asked myself. Running, baking, reading, speaking, blogging.

Keen to take control of my day (and my life!), I got up, laced up my trainers and hit the road. Running is the best way for me to get out of my head and back into my body – back to the present moment. It was early and there were a lot of cars on the road as people headed to work. I remember thinking to myself, 'I'm so glad I don't have to go to work' and then, 'Huh, that's funny – I couldn't say that just two years ago.' As it began to rain and the wind picked up, I smiled and thought, 'Good, this will clear my head.'

I was listening to a motivational video on YouTube – a mash-up of motivational messages taken from films and interviews with speakers, actors and celebrities and the stories were getting me pumped. I jumped in the puddles, letting the cold rainwater soak through to my socks. 'Who cares?' I thought, 'Trainers can dry.' I was on a high – leaning into the hills, powering myself up with my arms repeating over and over, 'Don't quit on yourself, Lisa, if you can make it to the top of this hill, you can make it to your dream life.'

I realised, listening to those speakers, that the world doesn't give you what you want, it gives you what you deserve. The world will not accept a payment plan for the life you want. You have to pay up front and in full. I knew what that meant: the Universe wants to help you, but you must do your share of the work. How can it deliver you a book deal if you don't have a book?

The Law of Attraction is perhaps one of the most important things we need to understand and practise when building our dream lives. You can't just work your way to your dream life. Trust me, I've tried that. You can't just dream your way to it either. I've tried that, too! In order to build your dream life, you must keep your goal in focus, direct your thoughts to what you want, act on the inspiration that comes to you but release your grip on the *how*. You must remain open to the possibilities and able to welcome them when they come. Half of the challenge in working with the Law of Attraction is learning to receive.

Right action, right mind, as Wattles taught us.

Focus on what you want

What I've come to realise is that most of us do the opposite of this. We focus on how much work there is to do, we wake up in a fear mindset and we work from a place of panic and lack and not from a place of abundance and joy.

Let's say you want to manifest more money in your life. You say things like 'I want to be a millionaire' but the thought seems so far out that you actually put yourself in a state of lack. 'Surely, that's not possible,' you affirm to yourself. You go through your bank accounts. You add up what you owe. You worry about where you'll find the money for a big bill. And the thoughts linger in your mind all day, manifesting more debt, more bills.

You get on a call with a prospective client and you're in fear, you're worried about money: You **need** this sale! Clients can feel that and it's not very appealing.

Contrast this with an abundant mindset. You wake up, you make a note of all the things that are flowing to you and all the opportunities you have. You write down what you're grateful for in your life and say things like, 'I can't wait to have more money' and 'I'm excited to pay that bill I owe'. Later, on a call with a prospective client you are confident, abundant, you exude creative energy. You trust that the solution is coming. This energy is very appealing, and the client says yes!

You see, the vibration for abundance and the vibration for lack are polar opposites. You can't feel lack and manifest money and you can't feel abundance and manifest lack.

Swoosh… A lorry drove past a little too close to my left arm. The wind pushed me into the gutter and it brought me back from my train of thought: I'd been writing in my head as I was running. Ideas, sentences and whole chapters played out with each step and I was writing this chapter.

Then something weird happened. I had a sort of vision of my future self. I could see myself in twelve months' time – published, fit, happy, speaking on stage and doing what I loved. I had a lovely new black car and I was baking every day in a beautiful big open kitchen. Running uphill, soaking wet from the rain and panting from the incline I pointed into the future stating, 'I see you, Lisa, and I'm coming for you. I am you. Thank you!'

It occurred to me that everything I have today, the woman I am today, is thanks to the intention I had set twenty-four months prior. It was thanks to the big, bold, brave actions I'd taken to change my life. I had become my vision.

My life was the sum of the new rituals I had built. My body was a reflection of my running and my new meat-free diet. My new clients had come to me because I had launched my dream business and told my story. I was over depression because I had learnt about chemicals in the brain – I'd quit coffee and I was being true to myself.

These things don't happen overnight. They build, over time. You become what you do every day. A vision will only come true if you act, today, as if it were inevitable.

'Thank you, Lisa!' I shouted in the rain. '**Thank you**!' I reached the end of my run, flung my arms in the air as if I was entering the stage to deliver this as a talk and I cried. I let it all out. Then I walked home, fired off only the urgent emails and invested the rest of the day writing this book and working on my online course. This is what they mean when they say, 'Do something today your future self will thank you for'.

You are made up of everything you have or haven't done so far. Your vision isn't your future: it's the life you're building right now. So, let me ask you again:

1. What do you want to be celebrating twelve months from today?

2. How do you want to feel each day?

3. Who are you here to become?

4. What do you want to create in this world?

5. *And what are you going to do about it, today?*

What you think about, you bring about.

PART THREE

HOW TO MAKE A LIVING DOING WHAT YOU LOVE

SEVEN

Your First Sh!t Version

So... the creative process is ugly as F. Let's just get that out of the way. It's the reason so many people never begin 'that project' and why so few finish anything at all. We have a need to be perfect. We were taught that there is one right answer. We want people to like us.

You are a creative being

We have a tendency to think what we produce is final, permanent, like it must stand alone. That's just not the case. You can write another book and form a *body* of work. You can make a *series* of videos and get your message across in multiple ways. You can develop your message *over a year* of posting blogs rather than trying to say it one piece.

To be creative – to be truly creative – we have to let go of our need for perfection and accept:

- Your first version will most likely be shit (but not as shit as you think).

- What you're creating is so unique there *is* no model of what is 'right' or 'wrong'. It just is.

- The people you know will not be the people who buy from you, so their opinions are pretty useless anyway!

- You won't know what it is until you start building it. Things are built through action and iteration. And sometimes 'one book' just isn't enough.

I'm laughing as I type because I've lived by these principles for ten years and it's why I've been able to launch three six-figure businesses in the last decade. It's why you're reading this book. It's why DARETOGROW, the movement, even exists. I launch when it's helpful to people who need it, not when it's perfect for the critics who judge it.

I just accept that the first version of anything I do will be pretty shit. I follow my heart and not my head. And I build what I want to build knowing that the right people will be attracted to it, rather than doing anything for approval. The commercial aspect comes later, as I will explain in Chapter Eight. Let me tell you something important: *you have a unique gift to bring to the world and no-one can do this or take this from you.*

I mean no-one could beat Beyoncé to being Beyoncé could they?[1]

There is no competition, no threat and no rush. Only the hasty excitement that comes with introducing new ideas, new services and new ways of working to the world. The more you share, the more the Universe will move through you. You have to make room for the next version of your 'thing' by releasing the seed of it into the world.

Have you ever noticed that when you act on your inspiration and start sharing your ideas with people, opportunities arise, seemingly from nowhere? A friend asks to help. You visit a venue quite by accident and it's perfect for your event. You receive an invitation to be on a podcast of someone you follow online? It's because there is energy in your action.

Plus, I have to tell you: your idea of the thing (the vlog, the book, the course) will always be better in your head than your ability to produce it in real life. That's why it's called a vision and that's a tough pill to swallow.

So take the pressure off for a second. The first version does not have to be perfect. It just has to be good *enough* to move you through to the next stage. It just needs to be done *enough* for people to consider it. It just needs to

---

[1] And can I just note: Beyoncé is so famous that my spellchecker highlighted her name to prompt me to add the accent to the *e*.

be helpful *enough* for it to help people. Price accordingly, press send and get to work improving V2.0. That's what I mean when I say, 'Put out your First Sh!t Version.'[2]

When inspiration strikes, act

Let me take you back for a moment to tell you how DARETOGROW began...

It was Autumn 2015 in Manchester and I found myself lying under the large white Ikea tables we had in our living room. I felt tormented. Depression clung to me. The debt was choking me. And the way out felt daunting. Not only did I have to pay off tens of thousands of pounds in outstanding debt, heal mentally, and readjust to my new life without blinkers, I also had to pay my way *today*.

I knew I had a choice: stay doing what I was doing (building websites and marketing for large corporates) and pay off the debt. Or, take a risk: do the work *while* building something new in the meantime. Take a punt on my real dreams. Put my money where my mouth was.

---

2   I'm laughing as I type because there is a term in product development called an MVP, or minimum viable product. It's the most basic version you can arguably sell to the customer and the purpose is to test your idea before you invest too heavily in the fancy bits. I guess you could call your First Sh!t Version – an FSV.

The 'something new' was to become DARETOGROW. It felt like a slab of concrete on my chest. Could I really write talks and inspire people to change their lives? Look at the state of my life. Could I really build an online course teaching people what I knew? All I'd done up until now was share other people's content. Could I really make a living doing what I love? I knew how to invoice for websites. But coaching? Really?

Alice coaxed me out from under the table and said, 'Lisa, you need to get on a run.'

She was right, of course. Creativity never comes from fear and self-pity. Creativity comes from space, inspiration, positivity – movement.[3]

I dragged myself from under the desk, pulled on my trainers and left the flat with a motivational speaker playing in my ears. I ran to the park. 'Bumped into' other people's dogs so I could get a quick dog cuddle. And I cried. Because this is how *purpose* feels sometimes; like a burden you're not ready to carry.

People like to paint it as a beautiful truth – a light fluffy ball of fuzzy creativity that just appears, magically before you. It is, ultimately – but we need to pass

---

3   There has been many a moment when writing this book that I've stopped. I couldn't seem to write another word. Sitting around is not a cure for that. So every time, I'd get the dogs and we'd go for a walk to the beach. By the time I'd returned home and made a tea, I was ready to go again.

FIRST SH!T VERSION

through the ego to experience that. And that requires growth! Purpose, then, is growing into your truth. Purpose means letting go of what's expected of you to follow your calling. Purpose is being *you*, not pacifying *them*.

As I walked home, I asked myself a question: *'What are you trying to do here, Lisa?'*

I was still running my marketing agency (now a team of one!) and I'd just sold my shares in the recruitment company.

This is what I knew: I wanted people to feel inspired, no... empowered, like their dream really was possible. 'Show, don't tell,' I thought to myself. I wanted the freedom to live, work and travel all over the world, so I knew it had to be online. A course? YouTube videos? A membership site? I knew I wanted it to be more than a business. I wanted to build a movement; accessible to anyone and everyone who wanted to change their life and change the frickin' world.

I skipped back into a run, ran home and burst into the living room.

I took out a massive sheet of white flip chart paper. I tipped out the jar of coloured pens and I started mapping out my strategy for DARETOGROW.[4] It included

---

4   And can I just add here that I had no idea what I was doing. I'd never built an online course. I'd never filmed a video series. I'd

weekly posts to inspire people, it included vlogs to document my journey of change and it included an online course to fund the endeavour.

Making money from your purpose

And here's the thing: *you're allowed to make money from your purpose, from your gift.* In fact, it's imperative that you do. If you have been called to share a message with hundreds or thousands of people and your intentions are good, then you're going to need some things to help you achieve your purpose: a team, infrastructure, budget for marketing, learning, coaching.

We have been taught a form of commerce that is competitive and limited. That for one person to win, another person must lose. But that's wrong. As I grow in wealth, reach and opportunity, I do not and should not stop another person from attaining what they desire, too. In fact, what better way to achieve these things than by *helping* others to attain what they desire? As we live out our true purpose, we lift other people up. If that's not the case, it's not your purpose: it's the ego mind.

Purpose lifts up. Ego locks down.

'I'm waiting to see what my boss says.'

---

never sold something 'online' before. I was totally green. I started from scratch and you can, too.

'It's the government's fault.'

These are thoughts that lock us down.

'I can have, be, do anything I want.'

'I'm learning a new skill.'

These are thoughts that lift us up.

Nowhere must we take more responsibility for our own lives than in the creation of our independence so that we can more fully express our gifts. This is why I am so passionate about teaching people how to build purpose-driven businesses. When you're in the driving seat of your life, when you have the money to share your message, when you have the freedom to choose how you spend your time, you can be more, do more and share more, according to your purpose.

Wattles' book, *The Science of Getting Rich*, is the ultimate guide to this. In fact, I love his book so much I now send a copy to everyone who joins Expansion Business School.

Chapter after chapter he talks about getting rich. He believed it was important to attain riches to fully express our gifts, to feed our minds and to help others. Our purpose here on earth is to be ourselves, express ourselves fully and make the most of ourselves.

He wrote in Chapter Five, titled 'Increasing Life', '… you are going to get what you want, but in such a way that when you get it every other man will have more than he has now' (p34).

And this is the secret to business, to success and to wealth: leave everyone you meet feeling like more is possible for them. Teach them how to tap into their power. Show them how to tap into their own power to rise up of their own accord. This is how to change the world: change lives.

That night, after my run, I mapped out my online course. It was to be six weeks long, with one video per week. The idea was to release one video on the Monday and then go live in a private Facebook group or via a webinar to discuss the 'homework' that Sunday.

A few days later, I walked back into the flat after a client trip to London. I was exhausted. Not from driving the Peugeot 107 up the M1 so late at night,[5] but from thinking and rethinking about my idea. Sometimes you just reach the point of exhaustion with an idea and the only cure is *action*.

It was 12am. Alice was heading to bed.

'Are you coming?' she asked.

---

5   Which at this point was so beat up, it would no longer go into first gear. The poor clutch was doing a lot of work on hills!

'No, I don't think I am,' I replied. We both knew what I was about to do.

I set up the tripod and the handicam my parents had bought me for Christmas. I tidied up the books on the bookshelf in the spare room – my soon-to-be filming backdrop. I flicked on the lights I'd bought in the sale in town.

Then – alone and in the dead of night – I filmed the First Sh!t Version of my course. The themes? How to uncover your purpose, how to change your life and how to make a living doing what you love.

I edited the first one that night and uploaded it to YouTube, marking it as 'unlisted'. I created a 'worksheet' by adding questions to a PowerPoint page and exporting it as a PDF. It was perfect...*enough*. And I began selling the course the next day.

I sold six places at £39 in my first launch. Most people would have been disappointed, but I wasn't. I knew if I could sell six spots, I could sell ten. If I could sell ten, I could sell one hundred.

And I did.

In the months and years that followed, I launched and relaunched that course, making it better and better with every launch.

Two hundred pounds in sales turned into two thousand pounds in sales.

Two thousand pounds in sales turned into ten thousand pounds in sales.

And before long, I was running multiple five-figure launches.

In just under four years, I built DARETOGROW into a national brand, generating hundreds of thousands of pounds annually from online course sales and a group coaching programme. I built a team, I rented an office, and dramatically increased the volume and quality of free content we shared online. And I got to travel all over the world, I overcame depression and I experienced a feeling of abundance like no other. At no time did I know exactly what I was doing! I was just walking blindly but boldly into the dark corridor of creation. I held my vision strong and I took one small step every day to bring my vision to life.[6]

Have patience

But I want to highlight something here people don't always see. People who've followed me online for a

---

6   Version 10 of my workbook for The Online Course is epic! I look at it now and know I could never have created that overnight. I feel like creativity is cumulative. First Sh!t Versions can grow into truly outstanding things of beauty!

while see me doing lots of things: I make videos, I write articles, I've launched a podcast. But I only have two core products. I have an online course and I launched it six or seven times before I had my first £10,000 launch. And it wasn't until I'd completed ten launches of that online course that I launched my group coaching programme – Expansion Business School.

I was patient. I put in the time. And I kept myself afloat from the wages in my marketing agency before I leapt fully into DARETOGROW.

I cried. There were nights of no sleep. And when I said *no* for the first time ever to a £5k web project, I smiled to myself: 'You've done it, Lisa, you've bloody done it.' What I built in DARETOGROW was unique. It was powerful. I didn't just ask what people wanted or needed, I built what was in my heart. And that was unique. I didn't just look at other coaches for inspiration. I read books on sports, fashion and cooking! And that was innovative. I didn't just focus on the money. I built a workbook that cost a fortune. I made welcome boxes that took days to ship in batches. And that was personal.

I went in with the idea that I wouldn't just make money. I wanted to make money and inspire others to make money of their own. I wanted to make the world a better place by showing people they could overcome depression, get out of debt and make a living doing what they love. And because of that I didn't just build a business – I launched a movement. No movement is perfect. You don't set out to build it one day and it's done the next day. It takes time to build a business and make a living doing what you love. It takes time to learn the skills you need to market and sell your offering. It takes time to clear the blocks and raise your consciousness. If it's not a mindset block, it's a skillset shortage. If it's not a skillset issue, it's a mindset block! Each new level requires a development of both. And in the meantime, the First Sh!t Version will do. And then the next shit version. And the next.

So, what do you feel called to create? Is it an event for mums? Is it freedom for people who've been hurt? Is it justice for people who need help? Is it a course or a programme for business owners? Is it classes? Is it a change in the law?

I have a feeling you already know.

What does it look like? If you were to pull out a sheet of paper or start a new document or type it in notes on your phone, what would be the first *shit* title? The first *shit* outline? The first *shit* approach? If your days were numbered on this planet and you had to share what you knew in a way people could learn it, how would you do it? If you had to launch it next Friday, what would you put out into the world?

Don't stop flow to check details

Give yourself time, today if you can, to answer these questions and map out your First Sh!t Version. Don't edit as you go, map it all out from start to finish and then go back and improve it later. Or better yet: launch it! And improve as you go. Improve through feedback. You know what they say: a shit version that's out there is better than the perfect version in your head. Wait, do they say that?

When writing this book, I wrote and rewrote whole chapters and even whole sections.

Sometimes I'd come back after a day and improve a chapter. Sometimes I'd come back a whole six months later and wonder, 'What was I thinking?' I'd laugh, and try again, culling whole chapters.

Each new draft felt like a drastic improvement on the last, but here's the thing: you can't 'redraft' something that doesn't exist; you can't rewrite something that's still in your head.

My best tip? Write and don't stop. Just write the whole chapter (or script or agenda or talk) from start to finish. Don't stop to check quotes or get references. Don't stop to reread a paragraph or find a synonym. Just spill the whole thing onto the page. *Say* what you want to say; the essence of it. Just get that First Sh!t Version out of your head. And once it's done, make a yourself a cuppa, and then buckle in for version two.

Coming up with a name

Not long before writing this chapter (for the third time, ahem), I launched a group coaching programme and I didn't yet have a name for it. So I called it DARETOGROW – The Group Coaching Experience. That was the First Sh!t Version.

The name eventually came about on a ferry ride back from Europe in January 2019. I already knew I wanted to run a group of some kind; I wanted a 'follow on' from The Online Course (I still don't have a name for that either) – something more advanced for graduates and people already further on in the journey. I'd been sketching the outline on sheets of paper. I'd started building a landing page on my website to explain it. And I needed a name for it.

On the way back from Amsterdam, Alice and I felt amazing. We'd just spent a whole month travelling and running our businesses 'on the go'. We honestly didn't know until that moment if it were truly possible. It just seemed like a dream other people were living.

At breakfast, halfway between Amsterdam and North Shields Alice said, 'Make a toast.'

In that moment, I felt an immense feeling of *expansion* in our lives, like it was really possible to live and work from anywhere and we were now doing it. Without thinking, I raised my glass – a champagne glass filled with orange juice – and said, 'Here's to *expansion.*' The hairs on my arms stood on end. Alice's eyes widened, and she smiled warmly. Tears formed in my eyes.

'That's it,' I blurted, 'That's the name of my programme.'

She nodded, and we both sat in silence.

When I got back to the UK, I launched the programme – an online group coaching and business training programme for purpose-driven entrepreneurs. I priced it up. Finished the landing page on my website and did a series of Facebook lives to tell my community about it. One person joined, then another, then another! And before I knew it, more than a dozen people had joined the programme in less than two months.

Things evolve

As I started to work through the content with the new members, and as I hopped on calls with each person, I realised two things:

1. The length of the programme wasn't long enough to do this work.

2. People didn't just want *me*, they craved a
   community of likeminded entrepreneurs on the
   same journey as themselves.

I realised my clients needed time to do the work *and* to
know that they weren't alone: it wasn't a crazy under-
taking to try to make a living doing what they loved.

I made three changes:

1. I reduced the length of the original programme
   and gave people the chance to stay on in a
   membership style at a fraction of the price.

2. I designed workbooks with weekly and monthly
   goal sheets.

3. I announced a surprise mastermind weekend at
   my home in Tynemouth along with regular meet
   ups in major cities around the UK.

Everyone was delighted. And they hurriedly booked
their transport and made their plans to join me for a
weekend of strategy and marketing for the first ever
Expansion Mastermind. And I cannot stress enough
that when I launched DARETOGROW/The Online
Course, Expansion did not exist, not even as an idea
in my mind. And when I launched Expansion, I had no
intention of running mastermind weekends. One thing
leads to another. But you must always begin with the

first step; you must act on the idea to create a *container* for what is to come.

As everyone started to arrive on the Saturday morning, I welcomed them with a hug and showed them through to the open kitchen. We'd put fresh croissants and pastries in the oven to heat up. There were new white candles burning in every room, including the bathrooms (an important detail). There were flasks of hot water standing tall beside neatly arranged rows of homely mugs. The doors to the garden were flung open and sun poured in through the windows.

'Wow', they breathed as they entered the space. I could see them relax immediately, knowing they'd made the right decision to come.

Six months earlier, Alice and I had been house hunting. We had a clear list of requirements including: a feeling of space, abundance and luxury; plenty of room to host clients, parties, family; and friends and a room each where we could work on our dreams undisturbed.

We knew as we put down the deposit for this place – a five-bedroom home within walking distance of the beach in Tynemouth – what we would be doing with the space. Alice would be hosting moon parties for members of her monthly membership – *The Sisterhood*™ – and I would be hosting mastermind weekends, but I just didn't know what for at that point. 'Expansion' wasn't a thing yet.

Once everyone had hugged and said hello, I interrupted warmly, 'Welcome, everyone, to your mastermind weekend.' I motioned to the living room, 'If you'd like to top up your tea and make your way through, we'll begin.'

The group who'd been deep in conversation with the bodies of the heads they'd engaged with online for the past few months, topped up their cups, headed to the living room and chose their seats.

People had travelled in from Germany, Northern Ireland, Scotland, Somerset and Cornwall. The four corners of the UK and beyond. I knew they were nervous. I could tell from their questions, their messages and the way they came into the house. And the nerves didn't just come from the anxiety of new places and meeting new people. As we would later uncover, the nerves came from a place of uncertainty about their worth and the value they could add to the world: *am I ready to show up at this next level? Am I enough? Will I be found out?*

'This weekend,' I began, 'is a chance for you to think strategically about your business.'

I looked around the room and saw a group of excited but equally nervous faces sat in front of me. These weren't just clients. They were my *dream* clients. And they weren't just here to grow their businesses, they were here to reach for more happiness, reach for a bigger life, reach for their long-held dreams (the ones they'd kept secret for so long). And I was ready to show them it was all possible.

'This weekend,' I continued, 'I don't want you to worry about how you'll get more followers on Instagram or what ad to run on Facebook, I want you to answer one simple question: *how will you turn up in the world*?'

I paused and handed out a worksheet with six carefully crafted questions.

The candles flickered on the fireplace. The smell of the orange diffuser floated gently into the space from the room adjacent. Sasha, our whippet, turned and grumbled with pleasure in her bed underneath the flip chart, beside a wall of my favourite books, arranged by colour.

'Take a worksheet and pass them on. I'm going to give you ten minutes to answer these questions.'

Gentle piano music played in the background as the group sat in silence, pondering their answers. Once they were done, I invited each person to take their place at the front of the room and share their intentions. I was asking them to show up, to speak up, to share. And I'd created a space that invited and welcomed the truth.

That afternoon, following a vegan lunch I'd brought in from a local coffee shop and restaurant – run by my friend – I split everyone up into groups and set them a challenge.

That night, we shook off the work of the day and headed to my favourite curry house in Tynemouth, where we ate, chatted, laughed and washed it all down with a cheeky drink.

The next day, before the Sunday session, we met at King Eddie's Bay, a stone's throw from the house. In bikinis, costumes, shorts and wet suits, we ran screaming and laughing into the North Sea. We danced in the waves, shouted our visions out to the sea and enjoyed tea in paper cups on the shore.

Everyone was present, aligned, confident... and smiling from ear to ear. The atmosphere in the house, the purposefulness of the questions, the mindfulness of the swim, the connection with each other was designed to help them turn down the voices of the outside world and tune into the voice inside: the part of them that knows what to do. They were reconnecting with their purpose; their higher selves.

After a warm breakfast, a few hours of sharing deeply and a guided visualisation for good measure, I broke everyone into groups once more and asked, 'Now, how are you going to show up in the world?'

Everyone's chests rose as they took a deep breath, understanding the question more fully. I was asking them to find the courage to reveal their truth and to show up from a place of purpose. I was asking them to step into their role as leaders.

Of course, I couldn't just sit them down and ask them as soon as they walked through the door. People enter rooms in their ego mind – nervous, conscious and wanting to flee! I had to take the time to guide them back to the present moment; to help them reconnect with their purpose.

I knew in that moment that I'd done it. I'd figured out how to empower people to build purpose-driven businesses so they could make a living doing what they loved and change the frickin' world.

It was four years since the journey had begun.

Could I have planned that from day one, lying under that white table in Manchester? Absolutely not.

Did I need to? Absolutely not.

That night, I opened up my laptop and updated the title of the group coaching programme to Expansion Business School: *The Business of Purpose*.

Don't wait for perfection. Just get the First Sh!t Version out there this month and go from there. There is a group of people out there waiting for exactly what you were made to bring to the world.

EIGHT

The Business Of Purpose

Let's press pause on the ambition for just a second and get practical. I've read many a book that focuses on the grand vision and the bold possibility and I subscribe to that notion too.

But how do you get started? How do you make your first sale doing what you love? Well, when you first start out on this journey to make a living doing what you love, you're not really building a business; you're building a product; you're crafting your message; you're building a community.

In the beginning, you're really just having a stab at putting something out into the world that people might find useful. Turning it into a *business* with people, systems and processes comes later. You need a product to get you moving.

It's why I don't recommend you quit your job to do it. If you asked me, I'd tell you to keep your job or keep the side hustle, so you don't have to think about money when building your First Sh!t Version. Remember that I continued to take on marketing clients and build websites while building DARETOGROW.

So, let's pause on the idea of building a big badass business just for a second and focus on the idea of putting your *thing* out into the world and getting people to consider it and buy it first.

Three things you'll need

There are three things you need to start selling your product or service and make a living doing what you love:

1. A clearly defined offer

2. A clear understanding of who you're trying to help and how to speak to them

3. Knowledge of where to find your customers

Let's take each one in turn.

A clearly defined offer

Wait, Lisa! You just said we don't need it to be perfect! Now it needs to be well defined?

I know, I did just say that. But just because it's not *perfect* doesn't mean you don't have to explain it!

If there is any confusion, people won't buy. And it's not *their* job to figure out what you've built or why it can help them. It's our job to do that. We must tell them what it is, how it meets a specific need they have and why it's more suited than other offers out there.

The best way to do this is to craft an offer that people can buy right now. Think of it this way. Let's say a friend recommends you to me because you're doing interesting work. I call you up to find out more. Can you tell me what it is? Is there a link I can click to find out more? And is there a way for me to sign up and give you money right now?

When I work with clients, I like to bring this altogether in a format called 'a landing page'.

A landing page is a page on your website that tells viewers all about your offering. Typically, it includes:

- An outline of what it is, eg *This is a three-month group coaching programme for purpose-driven entrepreneurs who want to build multiple six-figure businesses.*

- An indication of who it's for, eg *This is for you if you're excited to build a scalable business, you are heart-centred and you're already earning £30,000 in your business. This is not for you if you're looking for a quick fix, you won't turn up for the calls or you're not willing to try new things.*

- A list of what's included, eg *This course includes five one-to-one calls, weekly group coaching calls, a mastermind weekend, and so on.*

- Why they should buy it, eg *This programme is unique because it teaches purpose-driven entrepreneurs how to build a scalable business and avoid going through the pain of the boom to bust months.*

It could also include:

- Testimonials from other clients

- Any credentials you have for teaching this programme

- The price and any payment plans

- Specifically, what the client needs to do next to find out more or sign up

As my mum would say, 'Lisa, if people are on your web page, presume they want to buy. So, give them what they need to say "yes".' My mum has worked in sales for over twenty years. And she's the best![1]

Of course, it doesn't need to be a landing page on a website. It could be a slide deck, a well-crafted email, a store on Etsy, a market stall. The point is you must have a *store front*, stocked with things you can sell and a way for people to buy.

A clear understanding of who you're trying to help

This is one the things I spend most of my time helping clients with in the beginning.

When I ask them, 'So who are you trying to help?' I will often hear, 'Well, anyone can use it. I'm going after this sector and that one and this one too...'

For example, I had a client who wanted to be a life coach. He said anyone would benefit from life coaching whether they wanted a business or not and whether

---

1   Experience counts too. I really believe that if you've moved through something like debt, depression, anxiety or illness, you have wisdom you can pass on to people further behind you on the journey. I recently invited my mum on the DARETOGROW podcast. For weeks she messaged me saying, 'I can't wait to be on your *quadcast*, Lisa. Can you send me the question you're going to ask me?' She might be queen of sales, but she'd never done a *podcast* before, I mean a *quadcast*.

they were a start-up or an established business owner turning over six figures.

He was right of course; anyone *can* benefit from life coaching. But clients aren't 'anyone'. They're one person at a time and they want to know that your offering is *just right* for them, Goldilocks style.

Think about it for a second.

Let's say I'm in the market for some coaching. I feel stuck! And I want someone to tell me what to do next in my business. While I might loosely call it coaching, aren't I really looking for a business coach? Specifically – someone who has experience in making sales online? Someone who can guide me on the next step of my journey because they've walked the same path?

So, I get online and I find one coach who has some corporate pictures of himself in a suit. His service looks amazing and he says he can help me no matter what stage I'm at. He lives in the UK and is mostly present on LinkedIn. He specialises in helping people hit their goals. He also consults with companies and is the 'go to' coach on numerous boards.

Then I find another coach. She works mostly online and travels all over the world, with her dog Rascal (who I also follow on Instagram). She runs an online coaching business specialising in helping purpose-driven entrepreneurs uncover and remove the self-limiting beliefs holding them back so they can take the next step. She's a speaker and hosts a podcast, which I can listen to for free.

Who am I most likely to follow and who am I most likely to call?

There are so many clients out there who could really benefit from what you offer, and you will have a lot more success by speaking directly to them as individuals rather than talking loosely to a crowd.

Plus, people buy from people they know, like and trust. It is no wonder that the majority of my clients (easily 75% of them) have dogs and want to build online courses. People look for role models. They follow people who inspire them because they show them that their dreams *are* possible!

Look, someone is doing it in a town near me! It's possible!

So you have to be clear: who is your dream client? Who would be perfect for this programme? Who are you designing it for and why?[2]

---

2   This is where people say to me, 'Lisa, my dream client can't afford me.' This is direct: they're not your dream client. Your dream client should be able to afford your services. If they can't, be sure to share content they can access for free while they get in a position to choose you.

Once you have an idea, dig in some more and ask these questions to really get to know where they are and what they need:

- What do they crave more than anything?

- What feeling are they seeking?

- What do they worry about as they fall asleep?

- What guidance are they searching for?

- What do they need to believe about you to trust you?

When you know this, you can speak directly to the people you're best able to help in your marketing and in your sales conversations.

Knowledge of where to find your customers

When you know exactly *who* your clients are, you know *where* to find them.

I was advising a friend a few months ago. She said she wanted to work in the hospitality sector, advising people on their service.

'Hospitality?' I said, 'What does that mean?' I was also wondering what she meant by service – customer service? Table service? Room service? But, one question at a time.

'You know, pubs, restaurants, spas, hotels, those kinds of places.'

I looked at her with curiosity and asked, 'So who's the person who says yes and signs the cheques?'

'Well – it's different in each one. In hotels, it's probably the HR team, in spas it could be head office, in pubs – the owner I guess.'

I told her that was a lot of people to market to, before asking, 'Where can you go to find those people?'

She laughed and said, 'Yeah, I guess I'd have to go all over the place!'

Wouldn't it be easier to pick one sector to begin with and design a service that speaks directly to the buyers in that sector? Not only is it easier to 'speak to' your target customer but it's easier to get in front of them.

I think this is an exercise we can all give more thought to, even if we're doing well in business already. There is always more we can do to hone our offer, define our ideal client and communicate our offering more clearly.

Will you be here in five years?

Like I said before, just because it's your purpose, doesn't mean you have to do it for free! Your purpose is to be the fullest expression of who you are. People value that. And one of our biggest tokens of value is money. We need money to live, to explore, to grow, to experience culture. There is nothing wrong with earning money and in fact it's essential.

Think about your mission. You're not just here to help one person, are you? Or five or ten? I bet you want to help hundreds, thousands even.

Guess what? You need a dollar or two for that! You need money for lots of reasons: hiring a team, marketing to new audiences, building a brand. And if you want to reach hundreds and thousands of people, you'll need to set up a scalable system of value creation so you can deliver a consistent service to your clients time and time again.

Making money in business is important. Especially when you're purpose driven. Your mission matters even more.

A system of value creation

So, what's your plan? How are you going to do it?

The fancy business term for 'plan' is strategy – it originates from the Greek term for general, meaning leadership – and it means having an approach for achieving a goal with the resources, time and landscape available.[3]

Cynthia A Montgomery writes in her book *The Strategist*:

> 'It's a *system of value creation, a set of mutually reinforcing parts*. Anchored by a compelling purpose, it tells you where a company will play, how it will play, and what it will accomplish' (p72).

Ooh I love that!

So, imagine, if you will, that you're on one side of the river and your vision is on the other side. There are lots of ways to cross the river, right? You could use the stepping stones, take the bridge, fly a plane, and so on. But would you agree that you can't use the stepping stones and take the plane at the same time? It's impossible. They are all different approaches using different resources in different ways. But people try to do it *all* in business *all* the time. Heck, I've tried myself!

---

3   I love etymology – the origin of words. When you know where a word comes from, you have a deeper understanding of its meaning. It was in Cynthia Montgomery's book – *The Strategist* – that I learnt the origin of the word *strategy*.

People want to go out as a speaker *and* build an online course. They want to nail PR *and* become a vlogging sensation. They want to help large corporates *and* start-ups. Of course, you *can* do it all but as you start to scale, you realise every decision requires infrastructure.

Building a speaking career requires infrastructure. You'll need a showreel. You'll need to be networking and making new connections with event organisers. You'll need time to sit and write great talks.

Building a YouTube channel requires infrastructure. You'll need equipment. You'll need somewhere to film. You might even need a video editor.

When you're one person starting out with a dream, it helps to choose one key area of focus and give it your full attention.

So, pick an approach, pick a game plan and commit to it. Strategy is as much about what you rule out as what you rule in.

When I first started DARETOGROW, my strategy was to build an online course, launch it over and over until I nailed the sales process and make weekly vlogs to grow my brand. That's it! That strategy got me to six-figures.[4]

---

4   After six launches, I stopped running them *one after the other* and only opened the course twice a year. It made it feel more exclusive and it meant I wasn't online selling day in and day out. I could build

To grow to the next level, we changed our strategy. We introduced a group coaching programme called Expansion Business School and switched from vlogging to batch filming content that addressed questions six-figure business owners kept asking.

That got us to quarter of a million in revenue. And our strategy evolved again.

To make a living doing what you love as a teacher, a coach, a trainer, an artist, a chef... it's not enough to have a great product. You must have a *way* to bring it to the world that is unique and powerful. That is strategy.

How to build your strategy

I love that point Montgomery makes about strategy being a 'system of value creation'. I love the use of the word 'system' and I love the idea of 'value creation'. To be in business, you must add value to people's lives. The more value you can add, and the more people you can help, and the more scalable this is; the bigger your business and your impact can be.

The secret to making a success of your First Sh!t Version is to think it through strategically. Why does your company exist? How do you solve a specific problem

---

my brand, build community and then sell it into the people who'd been following me for a while. The trust was already there.

in a unique or special way? Or as Montgomery asks in her book: if your business were to stop trading today, 'would your customers suffer any real loss? (p7)'

To make it scalable is to ask how you'll turn your strategy into a system of value creation. This is about hiring people to help you. It's about developing processes, so the same thing happens each time, for each new customer. It's about introducing systems to take the pressure off people and make things happen automatically. People, systems, processes.

Keep this in mind as you answer these questions.

EIGHT BUSINESS QUESTIONS TO ASK YOURSELF

You won't know all the answers in reams of detail in the beginning. I believe the answers come through action; through interaction with your customers. So, let's see how far you get with these eight questions. Try answering them on a piece of paper today:

1. What am I trying to do here? (What is my vision?)

2. How will I know when I've succeeded? (What are the measures of success?)

3. Why does this matter? (What is the purpose of my business?)

4. Who am I trying to help? (Who is my target market or dream client?)

5. What specific problem can I solve? (What is the product or service I will introduce?)

6. How can I solve this specific problem in a unique and compelling way? (What will be my strategic approach?)

7. How can I do this exceptionally well? (How will I measure quality?)

8. What people, systems and processes can I put in place to scale this up? (What is the operational structure of my business?)

The mix of answers will create your strategic advantage.

For example, my vision is a world where any good person can make a living doing what they love. It matters because I want to help wake up more people in this world. I can't do it alone. So, I need to teach purpose-driven entrepreneurs how to build profitable, sustainable, scalable businesses so they can go out and do it too. I'm going to do this through a super-scalable online course and a next level business school. I'm building a team to do every single job that doesn't absolutely require my presence. I will go over the top in the value I add: bonus content, printed workbooks, live events etc so people rave about the courses and help me spread the word. I will share my story so people can see what's possible.

And I'll do it in jeans, T-shirts and denim shirts. Because that's me!

Any one of those things is copiable and has probably been done before. I mean, I'm not the first person to host a live event or create a workbook...or wear a denim shirt.[5] But the combination? That's unique. That's my *system of value creation*. And that's why people choose me. It's good fit for them and I can deliver the result they need. Your job is to be a good fit for the people you can help so they can invest in you with confidence. That is the business of purpose.

---

5   If it's not a denim shirt, you'll know it's a flannel one.

NINE

Why Clients Pick You

A few weeks before writing this chapter, I was in Manchester with my team. We were coming up to the launch of Cohort X – the tenth version of my online course teaching people how to uncover their purpose, change their lives and make a living doing what they love. I was in the offices and we were gathered around a computer, on a Zoom video call with our graphic designer who lived in the North East.

Hollie is super creative. You only have to give her one idea and she'll come back with a whole concept, story boarded out with actions within ten minutes. So I love speaking to her.

'I want Cohort X to feel special,' I said, 'I want it to feel like the launch of a big hit movie.'

Hollie laughed and said, 'Ooh Lisa, you should get your photo taken in front of posters around Manchester. Send them to me and I'll superimpose 'coming soon' graphics onto them.'

'I love it,' I replied with vigour. Once the call was over, I turned to my team and declared, 'Fuck it, let's do it right now.'

We put on our coats, headed outside and Amy in the team took photos of me in front of billboards and bus stops while Matt filmed it. It was a right laugh!

Heading back, I spotted a ten-foot sign on an island in a not-so-busy interchange. There was a bike chained to the railing beside it.

'One more,' I said, already halfway across the road.

Snap snap went the camera as I took the handles of the bike and pretended to get on.

That's when I saw the police car rolling up the street. I let go of the bike and rejoined my team.

'Keep walking,' I said.

We hadn't done anything wrong. I just know from experience that you tend to get moved on when you have a camera and cause a scene in somewhere like Manchester city centre.

The car turned onto the street we were on. I sighed. 'Ooops,' I thought.

The officers stopped the car and a man and a woman got out. Head to toe in uniform, complete with batons, handcuffs, radios. I admit, my heart sped up. 'What were you doing with that bike?' the female officer asked me with a stern and concerned look on her face.

'Erm, erm,' I stumbled, 'well, erm, I'm getting some photos for, I run a marketing agency, I, we just had ... '

I don't run a marketing agency! In my panic that's all I could think of. I mean how could I explain in a sentence, 'Well, I'm a business coach and I have this online course. We're doing a big, special launch and we had this idea to position it like a movie launch ... '

The officer burst out laughing, 'I can't,' she giggled, 'I follow you online and love your work!'

They pranked me! The coppers pranked me. I didn't know whether to laugh or cry. So I laughed. We all did.

'So that's how it is,' Amy summarised as we walked away. It was her first day in the business.

'I guess so,' I replied.

That's the first time anything like that had happened to me in a major city before – being noticed from my online content. People have stopped me in my hometown. I've had messages from people to say, 'I saw you in town today but didn't want to interrupt your day.' But this felt different. It felt like I was breaking through. I reminded myself of two things:

1. Always act in accordance with your truth because you never know who you're going to bump into.

2. Your work is changing the lives of people you will probably never, ever meet.

You see, you never change the world. You change lives: you change one life at a time. People forget this when they launch their first video online and only one hundred people watch it. Or they run their first event and only six people show up. We always think the numbers should be higher. We always think we're going to be the fluke that breaks through in three months and not four years.

In an era when people want to get there in ninety days, in a time when people make money by promising their unique webinar formula won them £100k of clients in seven days, in a time when there is so much BS, lean on *nature* for the truth.

Lean on nature for the truth

You can't cheat the growth process: you prepare the land, you buy the seeds, you plant the seeds, you look after the seeds, and your first season is, well, less then inspired. So, you go again and again and again, until a few years later you have a powerful wildflower garden, or a sapling of a tree.

Growth takes time. You know what else takes time? Marketing your business and building your brand, and here's why. You have to prepare the land first: you have to choose your arena and decide, this is where I'm going to focus my work. For example, I chose to focus on helping purpose-driven entrepreneurs. You might choose to help children or ex-military personnel or new mums or seasoned entrepreneurs.

Then, you buy your seeds. For me this means developing your knowledge, investing in your own personal development, building your first product. I've spent thousands, no, tens of thousands, on personal development. I've been on courses on how to write a book, how to use Facebook ads, how to grow your business. And each time I invest, I learn more things I can use and pass on to my clients. That takes time.

Then, you plant! You start telling people about the event or course. If you're really good in the beginning, you'll get some early interest and make a few sales. But in truth, the sales really start to build in year two, year three... years five and ten. Think about it. If you saw someone come out of nowhere with a fantastic new product or service, you'd be dubious right? Who are they? Where did they come from? It's human nature to sit back and observe – scrutinise – before we make a decision.

So how do you get around this? How do you build trust so people feel confident to invest in you? How do you build a community who will vouch for you?

You give away your best stuff up front, for free, and expect nothing in return... yet! Meanwhile, continue to grow and evolve. Live the life you're selling and show people it's possible because you're doing it. There is nothing more powerful than selling the life you're living.

And so, I built my course and I focused on brand, on integrity, on showing up! I shared vlogs every week to show my lifestyle changing. I wrote articles on how to change your life and how to make a living doing what you love. And when I went into my next launch, I even built a free mini course teaching people the best of what I knew. At the end I said, 'If you love this, then check out my epic new online course...' By that time, they'd seen me online for three months, they'd learnt from me and they felt confident I was real.

The freebie

I learnt this approach from an online mentor called Jon Penberthy, the British entrepreneur who has built multi-million-pound businesses teaching online marketing skills to people, largely through online courses. A lot of people have influenced my journey, but Jon has had a particular effect on me financially.

I first came across Jon through a Facebook ad (of course). He was driving in his car, telling us about the power of stories and teaching us what it takes to make sales online. There was something so genuine about him; something so different. I signed up immediately.

As the first video came through, I watched it and took notes. I was blown away with how much he was giving us for free. I loved how relaxed he was; showing us his life and bringing us about his day.

I actually remember being annoyed I had to wait a whole day for the second *free* video to arrive in my inbox. But sure enough it arrived. And then the third landed.

Following the free series, Jon invited us to consider his online course teaching us how to run profitable Facebook ads. I was so tempted to join but I simply couldn't afford it at that point. This was right at the start of my journey and I was beyond broke. I couldn't beg, borrow or steal another penny.[1]

So, I continued to watch him from afar, joining his webinars, scrutinising his ads and implementing what I could, based on his model.

I am certain that what Jon taught me in those free videos about 'putting on a free mini version of your offering' changed the game for me! It's an approach I follow (and teach) to this day.

And guess what?

In 2018, after following Jon for nearly three years and devouring all of his free content, I invested in his course. And I was glad to do it!

Customers don't always comment

Now here's the crux.

I watched Jon online for years before I invested. And I watched silently. I didn't comment much or engage. I just watched and learnt from afar. And as soon as I wanted training on Facebook ads, there was **one** place

---

1   I, of course, never stole any money! It's just a phrase and it felt incomplete as just *'beg or borrow'*. See? That just doesn't sound right does it? Back to the story…

I was going! Straight to his course! I couldn't wait to join. And he didn't disappoint.

I dived into the content in his paid course and implemented my learning immediately. I also participated heavily in the Facebook group we got access to as part of the programme. I wanted to give back and share what I'd learnt to help others just starting out.

I couldn't believe it when Jon messaged me to ask if I'd like to share my story on his stage at the next members' event. He wanted me to show people what I'd done, to remind people what was possible for them using this methodology.

It was a big fat yes!

I experience this a lot in my community, too. People join my paid programmes and when I email them to welcome them, I always hear, 'I've followed you for years and couldn't wait to join!' The funny thing is that I don't recognise most of the people who pay to join my programmes. Most of the people who pay to work with me have followed me quietly for years.

And the people who like and comment, who you think might join, rarely do. And there's nothing wrong with that either. Don't get too hung up on who joins and who doesn't. Just keep showing up. Keep adding value and making offers. Keep going.

If it's a fit, it's a fit. If it isn't, it isn't.

The message I want to get across to you here is the importance of committing to your vision for years not months, showing up consistently even when people aren't commenting, and launching again and again to build trust; to show people you're here and you will still be here when they're ready to join!

And that's why it's important to keep posting, even when it feels like no-one is watching. People are watching. And one day, after you put in your 10,000 hours, things start to change.

I learnt this approach from Joe Wicks, The Body Coach – the Londoner who'd made a name for himself with his *Lean in 15* range. One day, it seemed to everyone watching like he'd just blown up overnight! An overnight success.

He hadn't, of course, no-one ever does.

'Not a lot of people know this,' Wicks told Dan Masoliver from *Men's Health Magazine* in 2017, 'but I actually sent 20,000 tweets before I made a single penny off of social media.'

If you read about Joe's rise to fame, you will see him tell interviewers time and time again that he started with no audience and continued to post even when no-one was watching.[2]

---

2   Barney Cotton, '"My success wasn't intentional" Joe Wicks speaks on the importance of social media in business', *Business Leader* (2018), www.businessleader.co.uk/my-success-wasnt-intentional-joe-wicks-speaks-on-the-importance-of-social-media-in-business/43275

I must have really internalised this insight because over the next few years, I went on to make over 200 vlogs. My first fifty-plus were, you know, shit! But they started to get better and better.

As my business grew around the videos I shared online, I started to invest. First in a new camera – a Canon G7X at a whopping £500. Then a while later I bought a Canon 80D and a mic, to the tune of £1700. Then, I upgraded to Adobe Premiere Pro from iMovie. Then I hired a video editor. And on I go.

I didn't start with the cameras, the support, the skills. I built them – all – and it took years. But what I have now is solid. My brand means something. My business has systems and processes. We have culture. And it's scalable. Building anything – a forest, a bridge, a community – takes time. And the same is true of businesses and brands. They take time to build.

Consistency over volume

One of the questions I get asked a lot is, 'Which platforms should I choose and how often should I post?'

My answer is really simple: it is much better to post consistently and build influence on one platform than to post sporadically on multiple platforms and have no-one see your content. And, it's important that you love the content medium you choose.

For example, if you love writing, I'd definitely be writing long copy posts. If you love films and video making, I'd definitely be making videos and vlogs. If you love sound and the spoken word, opt for a regular podcast.

And contrary to popular belief, you don't have to do it all. You just need to create really good content and share it consistently. But here's the real trick. Don't be the adverts, be the TV show. This is by far the biggest thing I learnt from business owner, entrepreneur and marketing expert Gary Vaynerchuk.

Gary Vee, as he's more commonly known, broke the whole marketing model when he started putting out over two hundred pieces of content a day (nope – that's not a typo). This guy is everywhere, on every feed. And his model is super clever![3] He hires video editors to follow him around each day and 'document' what he's up to. His creative team then turns this content into daily vlogs. They extract the audio to make podcast content. And they pull sixty-second clips and screenshots to make video and graphic content for Instagram, LinkedIn and his other feeds.

It's impressive! And we do a smaller version of that at DARETOGROW HQ (shout out to my epic team!).

---

3   Gary Vaynerchuk, 'The Gary Vee Content Strategy: How to Grow and Distribute Your Brand's Social Media Content', garyvaynerchuk .com (2019), www.garyvaynerchuk.com/the-garyvee-content -strategy-how-to-grow-and-distribute-your-brands-social-media -content

What's important is that you enjoy the process of creation so you keep it going. If you hate writing, don't commit to writing each week. You just don't need to. Focus on what you love. Lean into your skills.

Be the TV show

When I first started vlogging, I had an intention. I wanted people to be excited to tune in and watch the daily videos. I hoped they'd fall in love with them as people fall in love with their favourite shows.

Each day I woke up, got dressed, picked up the camera and said, 'In today's video...' and I was off. For over two years, I filmed videos every week, staying up until midnight to edit them ready for release the next day.

People found the vlogs easy to watch and easy to share. I wasn't selling anything. It wasn't a gimmick. I was just showing my journey, telling the truth about how long it takes, and sharing advice on how people could make their next move, too.

As my business grew, I started using Facebook ads to put the video content in front of new audiences. Again, it was easy for people to engage because it wasn't an ad, it was a show.

At one point, I'd spent £2,500 over three months to put my videos in front of new audiences. A month later, I launched my online course and spent a further £1000 showing ads for the course to people who'd been watching my vlogs. I was genuinely shocked when I made £27,000 in sales a few weeks later.[4] It felt effortless. It felt fun. I had been doing what I love – sharing stuff about business, making videos, teaching – and when I made my offer, the people who'd benefitted from my free content found it easy to say, *'Hell, yes!'*, just like I did with Jon's course.

As Gary Vee says, don't be the ads, be the show.[5] This means create content that inspires, educates and entertains. Let people follow you, learn from you and grow with you. When the time is right and you launch a product or service, more people will know, like and trust you and you'll have credit in your bank to make a withdrawal. That's my interpretation of 'rent is due up front'. Lead the way for your community.

So – where do you begin? The best thing you can do to get moving with your content strategy is to ask one killer question:

What does my dream customer need to know to progress?

---

4   I want to stress here that I had been running and testing Facebook ads for over a year at this point. When I say, 'a few weeks later', this is on top of the time I'd spent building my audience and mastering the Facebook ad process. My spend increased with my experience in the platform.

5   Gary Vaynerchuk, 'How to Sell Anything on Facebook and Instagram', 4Ds Consultation with GaryVeynerchuk (2018), https://youtu.be/vSwIYTKTCgw

Take yourself away to a coffee shop, really sink into the mindset of your perfect client and list out titles to content that will genuinely help them move forward in their lives.

When I'm creating content for people who might join my twelve-week online course, I write titles like:

How to reconnect with your purpose now your children have left home

How to change your life ... when you think it's too late

The one thing I learnt from depression that set me free

When I'm creating content for potential clients of Expansion Business School, I write articles like:

How to hire your first employee ... when you think you can't afford to

How to have your first £10k month

You need to know this about strategy to scale to six figures

These topics will not appeal to everyone. But they will appeal to people I'd love to work with. And I wonder if one or two of those titles might have caught your attention?

Your right to teach

When I was eleven, I had a history teacher. Let's call him Mr S.

Mr S was so passionate about his subject. He came alive when he taught us about the Middle Ages, the Romans, the Great Wars. He would tell stories as if he was there. He would bring in costumes for us to see how people lived and really understand what happened.

I always remember him teaching us about *inflation*. He said that money wasn't worth the paper it was printed on and that during times of war, the value of money changed completely. This meant that one day you could afford bread with what you had, and the next you couldn't. He pulled out a twenty-pound note from his pocket, scrunched it up and threw it in the bin. Twenty pounds was a lot to us lot, sat wide eyed in his classroom wondering if he'd retrieve it.

Mr S had permission to teach us. We loved his stories and, while no-one would admit it at the time, we couldn't wait to hear more. If he was off sick and a supply teacher came in, not only were we disappointed, but we were concerned. Was he OK? Was he coming back?

When it comes to selling and marketing online, Seth Godin had it right when he coined the phrase *permission marketing*, in a book by the same name in 1999. Nearly twenty years later, he wrote about the same topic in his book *This is Marketing*.

'Real permission works like this,' he said, 'if you stop showing up, people are concerned. They ask where you went.'

As you build your audience online, you want to build up excitement, anticipation... you want *permission to teach*. So, while paid ads and paid marketing can help you reach more people, it doesn't buy you permission to communicate more deeply with them. You gain permission from adding value up front, from giving generously and from being true.

As Godin teaches us, permission isn't about getting someone to tick a box so you can market to them. Who's to say they'll read it? Who's to say they won't find it annoying? Permission is about making a deal with someone that you keep, ie if you sign up to my weekly mailer, I will send you more of this content. Deal? Deal!

Remember, it takes at least two to four years for most businesses to get off the ground. Some businesses get there sooner and some take longer, but that should give you a realistic starting point, so don't stop in month six or launch three. Keep going. Keep sharing. Keep asking for permission to teach.

Final Words – You Need To Calm Down

I hate the phrase 'goal setting'. It's so overused. How many times have we all set a goal and never hit it? It just makes you feel like a failure, right? The key to building your dream life is not to set goals but to get honest with yourself, to 'come out' as who you truly are and take actions aligned to that truth every single day. *Be the person you want to become today and let your dream life build around you in that present moment.*

Your dream life isn't something you move towards... it's something you build around you each and every day. In doing this, you don't wake up each morning closer to your dream life, you wake up each morning closer to who you really are. That's the goal that really matters. That's your dream life. That's fulfilment. In this essence, you don't really set goals at all. You take *guided action* every single day with the intention of becoming more aligned to your truth, to your soul, to your purpose. And that's the journey of life.

That's what I was merrily saying to Alice as we sat down to eat on the seafront at a café in Ibiza. We were there to run her first international retreat. Well, Alice was running it... I was there to support.

I continued...

'Do you see what I'm saying? You don't move towards your vision because tomorrow doesn't really exist. You pull it towards you by taking action today and becoming the thing you want to become. You want to be a writer? You gotta write today! You want to be a coach? Start coaching today.'

We were chatting away. Sharing our views on manifestation and building your dream life when the waiter, a lovely man named John, came over to ask how the food was.

Before he could finish his sentence, I was already moving my hand in the air in a signature motion – 'just the cheque please'. I wasn't being rude. I had started the motion as soon as I caught his eyes because I had eaten my food and I wanted to leave quickly. I was in a rush.

He stopped. Looked at me dead in the eye and said, 'Girl, you need to calm down!'

I looked back at him, came back to reality and burst out laughing. 'That might be the best thing I've ever heard,' I replied, 'I think you're bang on – I do need to calm down.'

I wasn't really in a rush. My energy was rushed. I was frantic from weeks in launch mode, tight timetables with flights and looming deadlines for various projects. We ordered two more drinks, sprayed on the obligatory factor fifty and sat back in our chairs to absorb the calming ebb and flow of the ocean.

Sitting there, watching a German Shepherd diligently chase a flip flop into the sea – I thought back on my journey.

Surrender is all there needs to be

It was January 2016, six months after 'the run' that was to change my life. I was tired, frustrated and fed up. Things weren't changing as quickly as I'd hoped. I'd already made the big bold decision to change my life and I was taking massive action to build my dream but, of course, the results were taking time. Following some initial momentum, I was still in debt, I was still overweight, and I was still stuck behind my laptop firing out emails and ticking off actions from my ever-growing 'to do' list.

Something wasn't working and I was growing impatient. I kept hearing the words of Oprah Winfrey in my head: 'It is understanding the surrender and that really is all there needs to be', but I couldn't fathom it, I didn't get it. I was in serious debt. Let go of what, I wondered? Surrender how, I asked?

Looking back over the last few years it all makes sense now. There does come a time when you have to let go and surrender, but it's not so much about letting go of life. It's about giving up the idea you're on the journey alone. Help is available when you open your arms to receive.

When I look back over the few years I spent paying off the debt, nothing bad ever happened to us. Yes, we were *threatened* by companies wanting to make us bankrupt. Yes, we were *threatened* with bailiffs, but the right amount of money did always show up for us just in time to keep on going. Plus, even if they had made me bankrupt, what does that really mean in the grand scheme of trying to live out your purpose and change the world? It would have been a serious lesson learnt but that's it.

What I've come to accept is that everything is always working out for each of us. Even when it doesn't feel like it is, it is. But I didn't know that then, as I awoke each morning ceremoniously reciting my actions for the day: reply to him, pay that invoice, complete that website. It was a never-ending list of fear-based actions.

At the time, I wrote in my journal, 'I feel really demotivated' with a real sense of despair, like things were never going to get better. 'Will I ever make it?' I asked myself.

I felt so low back then, so helpless. But what I've learnt on this journey is that was just my perspective. Feeling demotivated is not actually a bad thing. It's a sign from the Universe, 'You've drifted off course, follow your bliss and go *create* to get back on track!'

You see, I believe we all have a course in life. Not one that's mapped out in detail but rather one that we build when we take purpose-led, creative, source-driven steps forward in the direction of our vision for a better world. Your dream life is born from you, from the actions you take daily. It's intrinsic and it comes from within. That's why taking action based on intuition, inclination and gut feel is so important. We're being guided.

Feeling demotivated, then, is a sign that you're not taking guided action. Something is wrong, off-kilter. But that's OK – feeling demotivated is just one emotion on a very big scale. At one end of the scale, you might experience fulfilment – the feeling you get from living a purposeful life; the life you were born to live. At the other end of the scale you might experience depression – the feeling you get when you feel helpless; like all is lost forever. I've experienced both sides of the scale. I lived in a depressed state for six years of my adult life, from twenty-two right through to twenty-eight. I know where it came from now: it came from ignoring the signs, it came from ignoring my calling, it came from trying to blend in – fit in. I became so lost, so disconnected that I checked out of my own life. I mean that's what depression is, isn't it? Disconnecting from your life so you don't have to face it.

Depression is one coping mechanism, it's one way of checking out of our lives because we don't like how it's going or who we've become. Alcoholism and drug use are other mechanisms, so is over-eating, so is being angry all the time. There are others and we all have a coping mechanism – these coping mechanisms serve a purpose: they stop us from having to examine what went wrong. They stop us from taking charge of our lives and making the changes we really need to make. The big scary, disruptive changes that will flip your life 180°. The kind of changes I made in 2015 when I decided to give up my companies, take on the debt, come out as being a speaker... even though I'd never done any real speaking before!

What are the changes you've been avoiding? Do any come to mind?

When I used to run my live DARETOGROW events, there would always be someone who'd rush up to me and shout, 'Lisa – I've done it, I've quit my job!' or 'I'm moving to India.' I was always happy and terrified in equal measure.

'Is that OK?' I asked a mentor once, and she replied, 'No-one is doing anything they haven't wanted to do for years. You just gave them the confidence to do it!'

This is what this final note is about: realising that your life is not about the attainment of goals but the accepting of who you are. And sometimes you need to calm the F down to tune into that. When you find the courage to look inwards and remember who you really are, when you find the confidence to make that change, when you DARETOGROW and take action on your truth, that's when your dream life will unfold.

Getting over depression, giving up an addiction, changing your habits to build your dream life therefore takes a very special kind of courage. It's the courage to face who you are beneath the pain, the projections and the bullshit, to shout **I am Lisa Bean and I am a transformational speaker!**

Building your dream life is about giving in to that truth inside you; whoever you are deep down under the image you portray, behind the awards you've won and the successes you've achieved. It's coming out as who you truly are and taking actions aligned to that truth every single day. It's about living it. Today.

Goals, in some ways, can be a blocker to your dream life. They can bring you off course as you chase things that don't matter. All that matters right now is your intention to live your truth, to bring your story to the world.

I was not doing that aged twenty-two to twenty-eight. I was hiding, I was lying; chasing down big, stupid goals I only wanted to achieve to look good. When I hit them,

I never found the peace I wanted. I found depression because I'd come so far away from who I truly was that peace was impossible. I was split into two pieces. The version of myself I knew deep down and the version of myself I was presenting to the world.

One day I asked myself: *what if this situation wasn't as permanent as I thought? What if I stopped defending my depression and let it go? What if I could change my life by telling the truth; by living my truth?*

And this is why this next stage of this journey is the most challenging. You're going to have to get real. With me, with your family and friends and with yourself. Anyone can set a vision and fantasise about a new life but to actually make it happen you need to take some vital steps towards that vision, and those steps involve believing it's possible, acting as if it were guaranteed and trusting when things don't work out as quickly as you'd hoped.

This is where we set the goals that actually matter. The ones that are going to bridge the gap and make your dream life your new reality.

Imagine, right now, that you're back on the edge of that river. It's a fair-sized river – you wouldn't want to fall in – but it's crossable with a little ingenuity. Looking around you spot a pile of stones. Light enough to lift and big enough to hit the river bottom, forming a path you can cross. One by one, you pick up each stone and put it in the water. Then you come back, pick up another stone and, using the first stone you placed, move into the river and place the second stone. Then you come back for the third stone, and so on. Setting purposeful goals is like this. Just like you're trying to cross a river, stone by stone. Each stone is a goal or a project.

For example, there's no point worrying about stone three (the book deal) if you haven't written a book (stone two). Goals are progressive. Living a life of purpose is progressive. And it all starts with one inspired step today. What do you feel called to create? What gets you fired up and aligned? Which one small step can you take today on your journey?

Putting you first

Whenever someone stumbles or falls on their journey and says to me, 'Lisa, I'm lost' or 'I don't know where to focus', I always take them back to their vision. 'What are you trying to do here?' I ask them.

This is important because vision and 'day-to-day' are two separate things. Each and every day, we wake up and before we even look our partners, families and friends in the eyes, we're reaching for our phones, checking emails, counting the likes from our latest post. Then, we remind ourselves of what's on our 'to do' list. We recount the things we didn't do yesterday.

We remember the cups that are in the sink. And the puppy chewed the new cushion. And there is a letter you haven't opened yet. Am I close?

Day-to-day life can feel very overwhelming. It's so 'there'. Ping. Bang. Buzz. Things literally pop out of the screen, invading your space and **demanding** your attention.

Vision is different. Vision is up and out. It's forward. It's ahead. It's elevating. When you connect with your vision – not your to do list – and ask the following questions, you will always find a way to move forward:

- What am trying to build or create here? What key project must I therefore focus on this week?

- What do I want to be celebrating twelve months from today? Which one small step can I take towards that goal today?

- What am I trying to change? Therefore, where could I put my efforts in this moment?

- Who am I trying to become? What would that version of me tell me to do today?

- I am on a *journey* of change. What could I face today to change my tomorrow?

- Part of me knows what to do. So, if I had to guess, what are the next three steps, in order, and how can I take a step today?

Taking action isn't about waking up and replying to emails or checking Instagram. Taking action is a strategic decision. It's about putting your time, energy and focus into the projects, actions and decisions that will move you closer to your vision. And this is where my philosophy really holds its own.

No-one knows how to do this perfectly. Heck, when I first wrote this closing chapter, it was a mess. Unfinished sentences. Highlighted sections where I had to come back to find the actual quote. Incomplete ideas. But I learnt long ago that the key to writing is to write your full talk, chapter or presentation start to finish without stopping. Just **throw** it all on the page, literally. A stream of ideas, thoughts and words. Don't worry if it isn't perfect. Just get the overall structure, the key themes down. If you stop and reread every sentence, paragraph or page, you'll lose your thread, you'll lose momentum and you'll stop.

My first draft of this book was shit. But now it's finished. And now I can use it to further my cause. And, guess what? I just made room for book number two...

References

Bernstein, Gabrielle, 'How to Heal an Addiction', Gabbybernstein.com (2015), https://gabbybernstein .com/break-addiction

Bernstein, Gabrielle, *Miracles Now: 108 Life-Changing Tools for Less Stress, More Flow, and Finding Your True Purpose* (Hay House UK, 2014)

Bernstein, Gabrielle, *Super Attractor: Methods for Manifesting a Life Beyond Your Wildest Dreams* (Hay House Inc, 2019)

Brand, Russell, *Revolution* (Arrow, 2015), p54

Brown, Les, 'Step Into Your Greatness Live', YouTube (2013), www.youtube.com/watch?v=wo7leEPlEFY

Brown, Les, 'If you had six months to live …' YouTube (2019), www.youtube.com/watch?v=_sBMcuboHlY

Byrne, Rhonda, *The Secret* (Simon & Schuster UK, 2006)

Campbell, Rebecca, *Light is the New Black* (Hay House UK, 2015), p58

Canfield, Jack, and Switzer, Janet, *The Success Principles: How to Get from Where You Are to Where You Want to Be* (HarperCollins Publishers Ltd, 2005), p3

Carmody, Bill, 'Tony Robbins: I can tell you the secret to happiness in just one word', *Business Insider interview* (2017), www.businessinsider.com/why-tony-robbins -says-success-alone-wont-make-you-happy-2017-3?r= US&IR=T

Castro, Elizabeth, *HTML 4 for the World Wide Web* (4th edn, Peachpit Press, 2000)

Coelho, Paulo, *The Alchemist: A Fable about Following Your Dreams* (Thorsons – an imprint of HarperCollins Publishers, 2015), p viii

Cotton, Barney, '"My success wasn't intentional" Joe Wicks speaks on the importance of social media in business', *Business Leader* (2018), www.businessleader .co.uk/my-success-wasnt-intentional-joe-wicks-speaks -on-the-importance-of-social-media-in-business/43275

Dyer, Wayne, *You'll See It When You Believe It: The Way to Your Personal Transformation* (Arrow, 2005), p23

Eat Pray Love [DVD] Columbia Pictures (2010)

Ford, Henry, *The Reader's Digest* (The Reader's Digest Association, 1947), vol 51, p64

Gide, André, *Les faux-monnayeurs (The Counterfeiters)* (Nouvelle Revue Française, 1925)

Godin, Seth, *Permission Marketing: Turning Strangers Into Friends and Friends Into Customers* (Simon & Schuster UK, 1999)

Godin, Seth, *This is Marketing: You Can't Be Seen Until You Learn to See* (Portfolio Penguin, 2018), p190

Hicks, Esther and Jerry, *Money and the Law of Attraction: Learning to Attract Wealth, Health, and Happiness* (Hay House UK, 2008), p10

Holiday, Ryan, *Ego is the Enemy: The Fight to Master Our Greatest Opponent* (Profile Books, 2017)

Kaufman, Andrew, *All My Friends Are Superheroes* (Telegram, 2010)

Masoliver, Dan, 'Big Read: A day in the life of Joe Wicks', *Men's Health* (2017), www.menshealth.com/uk /fitness/a758121/what-mh-learnt-by-spending-a-day -with-joe-wicks

Montgomery, Cynthia A, *The Strategist – Be the Leader Your Business Needs* (HarperCollins, 2013)

Nichols, Lisa, 'How to Make an Impact by Standing ON Your Story, Not IN Your Story', YouTube (2012), www .youtube.com/watch?v=bsj26htBxr4

Oprah Winfrey Network, 'What Oprah Learnt from Jim Carrey', YouTube, Oprah's Life Class (2011), www.youtube.com/watch?v=nPU5bjzLZXo

Oprah Winfrey Network, 'Iyanla Vanzant on Surrendering to Your Purpose', YouTube, SuperSoul Sunday (2012), www.youtube.com/watch?v=ABCuZjs-8o8

Palmer, Parker J, *Let Your Life Speak* (John Wiley & Sons, Inc, 2000)

Penberthy, Jon, YouTube, www.youtube.com/channel/UCMK_SqoZtC43pZxwnfDFSlw

Robbins, Tony, 'The Key To Success? Model The Best', www.tonyrobbins.com/stories/unleash-the-power/the-key-to-success-model-the-best

Sincero, Jen, *You Are a Badass: How to Stop Doubting Your Greatness and Start Living an Awesome Life* (Running Press, 2013), p22

Sinek, Simon, 'How Great Leaders Inspire Action', TEDxPuget Sound (2009), www.ted.com/talks/simon_sinek_how_great_leaders_inspire_action?language=en

Singer, Michael, *The Untethered Soul – The Journey Beyond Self* (A co-publication of New Harbinger Publications and Noetic Books, 2007), p34

Stanford News, Steve Jobs' 2005 Stanford Commencement Address (2005), https://news.stanford.edu/2005/06/14/jobs-061505

The Matrix [DVD] Warner Home Video (1999)

Tolle, Eckhart, *The Power of Now: A Guide to Spiritual Enlightenment* (Hodder & Stoughton, 1999)

Tolle, Eckhart, 'Jim Carrey On The Power Of Intention', YouTube (2010), www.youtube.com/watch?v=8qSTHPABoHc

Vaynerchuk, Gary, 'The Gary Vee Content Strategy: How to Grow and Distribute Your Brand's Social Media Content', garyvaynerchuk.com (2019), www.garyvaynerchuk.com/the-garyvee-content-strategy-how-to-grow-and-distribute-your-brands-social-media-content

Vaynerchuk, Gary, 'How to Sell Anything on Facebook and Instagram', 4Ds Consultation with Gary Veynerchuk (2018), https://youtu.be/vSwIYTKTCgw

Ware, B, *The Five Regrets of the Dying – A Life Transformed by the Dearly Departing* (Hay House UK, 2019); blog, https://bronnieware.com/blog/regrets-of-the-dying

Wattles, Wallace D, *The Science of Getting Rich* (Capstone Publishing Ltd – A Wiley Company)

The Author

Lisa Bean is a UK transformational speaker and business coach.

Having launched three six-figure businesses, she now teaches purpose-driven entrepreneurs how to connect more deeply with their purpose, change their lives and make a living doing what they love, so they can change the frickin' world.

Keep up to date with Lisa here:
- 🌐 www.daretogrow.co.uk
- ▶️ www.youtube.com/c/DARETOGROWTV
- 📷 @daretogrowuk
- 📘 /daretogrowuk
- 🐦 @lisambean

Lightning Source UK Ltd.
Milton Keynes UK
UKHW022200070622
404067UK00008BC/1946